MAKING MUSIC

Essential Library

An Imprint of Abdo Publishing
abdobooks.com

BY SUE BRADFORD EDWARDS

abdobooks.com

Printed in the United States of America, North Mankato, Minnesota.
052024
092024

THIS BOOK CONTAINS RECYCLED MATERIALS

Cover Photos: Shutterstock Images (guitar, mixing console); Suradech Prapairat/Shutterstock Images (piano); Victoria Sergeeva/Shutterstock Images (music notes)
Interior Photos: Victoria Sergeeva/Shutterstock Images, 1 (left); Shutterstock Images, 1 (right), 30, 49, 73, 82, 85, 100, 101; Vladimir Vladimirov/E+/Getty Images, 4; Anthony Brown/Alamy, 7; Jasper Cole/Tetra Images/Getty Images, 10; Yan Cong/Moment/Getty Images, 13; The Picture Art Collection/Alamy, 16; Stefano Bianchetti/Corbis Historical/Getty Images, 19; G. Cigolini/De Agostini/Getty Images, 20; Michael Ochs Archives/Getty Images, 24–25; Chris Willson/Alamy, 27; Mas Jono/Shutterstock Images, 28; Dia Dipasupil/Getty Images Entertainment/Getty Images, 33; Scott Legato/Getty Images Entertainment/Getty Images, 34; Taiyou Nomachi/DigitalVision/Getty Images, 37; Kevin Winter/TAS23/Getty Images Entertainment/Getty Images, 40–41; Neilson Barnard/Getty Images Entertainment/Getty Images, 44–45; Simone Joyner/Getty Images Entertainment/Getty Images, 46; David Corio/Redferns/Getty Images, 50; Taylor Hill/Getty Images Entertainment/Getty Images, 53; Piotr Swat/Shutterstock Images, 56; Nattakorn Maneerat/Shutterstock Images, 59; Phynart Studio/E+/Getty Images, 60; Victor Lucas/Alamy, 62–63; Francesco Prandoni/Getty Images Entertainment/Getty Images, 65; Westend61/Getty Images, 69; Catherine Powell/Getty Images for CMT/Getty Images Entertainment/Getty Images, 70–71; M4OS Photos/Alamy, 74; Steve Granitz/WireImage/Getty Images, 77; Wahavi/Alamy, 78; NDZ/Star Max/GC Images/Getty Images, 81; Thaspol Sangsee/Shutterstock Images, 86; Andreas Rentz/Getty Images Entertainment/Getty Images, 89; Frazer Harrison/Getty Images for Coachella/Getty Images Entertainment/Getty Images, 92; Jonathan Nackstrand/AFP/Getty Images, 95; Christophe Archambault/AFP/Getty Images, 96–97; Mark Horton/Getty Images Entertainment/Getty Images, 99

Editor: Laura Stickney
Series Designer: Maggie Villaume

Library of Congress Control Number: 2023949558

Publisher's Cataloging-in-Publication Data
Names: Edwards, Sue Bradford, author.
Title: Making music / by Sue Bradford Edwards
Description: Minneapolis, Minnesota: Abdo Publishing, 2025 | Series: Making media | Includes online resources and index.
Identifiers: ISBN 9781098293369 (lib. bdg.) | ISBN 9798384912637 (ebook)
Subjects: LCSH: Music--Juvenile literature. | Music making--Juvenile literature. | Arranging (Music)--Juvenile literature. | Composition (Music)--Juvenile literature.
Classification: DDC 780--dc23

CONTENTS

A BUDDING MUSICIAN

Maya stood at the kitchen sink, humming to herself as she rinsed her glass and put it in the dishwasher. She needed to think of a gift to give her grandparents for their upcoming anniversary. The couple had recently moved in to an apartment and didn't have much space for new belongings, so Maya didn't want to buy them something new, even if she had the money for it. And the gift had to be especially awesome because her grandparents would be celebrating 50 years of marriage.

Maya always had a great time with her grandparents. The three of them often sang along to their favorite music in the car. They listened to music while making dinner too. Music was an important part of their lives. Maya was certain that her passion for music was a result of her grandparents' influence, and she wasn't the only one in the family who loved music because of them. Maya wanted to give her grandparents a music-related gift for their anniversary, and she knew exactly who could help her with this idea.

People interested in recording music can practice reading sheet music. This way, they can learn to play or sing songs they enjoy. Other musicians write their own music.

Maya hurried through the house to her older brother Graham's room. From behind his door, she could hear the muffled sound of his guitar. Whenever he was recording something, Graham hung a "Do Not Disturb" sign on the door. There wasn't a sign hanging there now, so Maya sent him a quick text. "Outside your door," she wrote. "Can we talk?"

Graham swung his door open. The walls of his room were covered with posters of his favorite guitarists. Between two posters stood a display case holding several guitars, and beside this was a guitar stand. Graham put his guitar on the stand and turned to face Maya. "What's up?" he asked her.

"I need an anniversary gift for Grandma and Grandpop," Maya said. "I want to record a song for them." She explained to Graham that she didn't want to compose a song. Instead, she wanted to record one of their grandparents' favorite songs, creating what Graham called a cover.

Maya was a high school freshman and sang in the school choir. She even sang an occasional solo. But she didn't want the recording to be simply her singing a song. That wasn't the kind of music their grandparents loved. Maya needed assistance because she didn't play an instrument. "Could you play with me?" she asked her brother.

COVER SONGS

Cover songs can be a great way for new singers and musicians to get their work in front of an audience. This is partly because the song is already written. The musician simply needs to learn it and play it. Some covers are very similar to the original recording. The musician can also add harmonies, alter the tempo, and make other changes to give the song an original sound.

Beginners can use entry-level audio editing software such as GarageBand, which comes preinstalled on Apple products. Users can record their own tracks or use premade instrument sounds to create songs.

14:23 Mon 10 Feb
Soul Organ
Track Pan
PLUG-INS & EQ
Compressor
Treble
Bass
MASTER EFFECTS
Echo
Reverb
Soul Organ
SLOW
FAST
ROTATION
GLISSANDO

> **Covers are amazing to learn for your own musicality [because] you are taking in all the tricks from Paul McCartney and Elvis Costello and Elton John and Train and all these amazing bands. You're offering new listeners a segue between something that they're familiar with and then your brand.[1]**
>
> ***—Jesse Daniel Smith, songwriter***

Maya could tell that Graham felt unsure about the idea, but she pushed forward. "I know it won't just be a gift from me if you play, but I thought it would be a better present if a group of us worked on it together," she explained. "It could be a cousins present."

Maya and Graham had several talented cousins. Maya knew that if they worked as a group, they could accomplish what she had in mind even if they weren't in a band together. Graham had been in a band for almost two years. He played the guitar and wrote songs. Fans had even watched his band's videos on YouTube. Maya and Graham's cousin Sammi was a drummer. She was in a band that played at weddings and fancy parties.

Their cousin Benji always said that he only tinkered on the piano, but Maya thought he was brilliant because he didn't need sheet music to play. Benji could read music, but he could also play a song on the piano after simply hearing it. He was in college studying to be a music teacher. Another cousin, Kimi, was in the same choir as Maya. She could sing harmony to just about any song she heard.

Graham agreed to help, so Maya quickly texted the group. The only person to answer immediately was Sammi, who agreed to help make the song. She told Maya she would work on contacting the others. But Sammi also brought up something important. They weren't all going to be in one city until the weekend of their grandparents' anniversary party. Sammi said they would have to find a way to combine separate tracks.

Maya didn't know what a track was. Graham explained that when a song is recorded, different instruments and singers will each be recorded on a separate track. This might mean the drums are on one track, the guitar on another, and the lead singer on a third.

Recorded as separate tracks, these individual recordings can be adjusted as needed. Then the tracks are mixed to create a single song. "If everyone makes their own recording and then sends it to you, I can show you how to combine them," said Graham. "But first you need to pick a song."

MULTITRACK RECORDING

Many musicians use multitrack recording. This involves recording different sounds on separate tracks. Vocals might be on one track, while drums or guitars might be on another. After recording, musicians can edit, remix, and adjust each individual track without affecting the other tracks. Multiple tracks can be recorded at the same time or individually. Sometimes music editing software comes with multitrack-recording tools. But people can also purchase multitrack-recording consoles.

Maya combed through Motown hits and made a list of songs her grandparents loved, including "Ain't Too Proud to Beg" by the Temptations, "I Heard It Through the Grapevine"

by Marvin Gaye, "Reach Out (I'll Be There)" by the Four Tops, "Please Mr. Postman" by the Marvelettes, and "Where Did Our Love Go" by the Supremes. Maya showed the list to Graham on her phone. "Which song do you think I should choose?" she asked. Graham listened to a few songs on Maya's list. Together, they selected "Ain't Too Proud to Beg."

RECORDING TRACKS

Later in the day, Graham helped Maya set up a microphone and headphones in his room to record her track. Maya looked at the bulky headphones and asked if she could just use her earbuds. But Graham told her that the headphones would produce better sound. They would allow Maya to hear exactly how her recording sounded as she was making it. The microphone stood upright on the desk. Graham told Maya not to rustle her sheet music or tap her nails on the desk, since the microphone would pick up those sounds.

Graham had an audio recording and editing program called Audacity pulled up on his computer. He had already recorded the guitar track for the song. Now it was time for Maya to make her own track. It took several tries before Maya was happy with her recording.

The first time Maya started to sing, the sound of her own voice surprised her. She thought it sounded different from normal. But Graham explained that this was how Maya sounded to other people. "You just aren't used to it," he said.

While recording, musicians often wear headphones to prevent bleed, or unwanted noise picked up by a microphone. They may also use microphone accessories such as pop filters to improve the quality of their sound.

On the next try, Maya stumbled over the song lyrics. Her third attempt went well. Maya felt a little nervous about sharing her recording with Graham and the other musicians in her family.

After Maya's recording was complete, she downloaded Audacity on her own computer. This way, she wouldn't have to use her brother's computer. The program was free too. Graham explained that both musicians and podcasters use Audacity to edit files.

When Maya opened her vocal track and Graham's guitar track, she noticed that they weren't the same length. Graham's file was longer. "You were probably nervous and sang a little fast," Graham said.

He showed Maya how to lengthen her recording using the tools in Audacity. She could change the tempo of her track, slowing it down without altering the pitch, which would lower her voice. Next, Graham guided Maya through the process of exporting the audio as a WAV file, mixing the two tracks to create a single audio file.

After she listened to their work, Maya uploaded the song to a file-sharing service and sent it to each of their cousins. Each cousin listened to it through headphones while playing or singing their own tracks. Then they uploaded their recordings. This kept everyone at the same tempo so that Maya didn't have to manually adjust the tempo of each recording on her end. This made it easier for Maya to align and merge the recordings.

Musicians who record music at home sometimes invest in special recording equipment, such as speakers and small mixing consoles.

WAV FILES

In 1991, the companies Microsoft and IBM created the WAV file format for saving sounds as computer files. The greatest strength of this format is that sounds retain their quality and are not degraded. The downside is that the files are extremely large. For each minute of play, the file is approximately 27 megabytes in size.[2] This is about 10 times larger than an MP3 file of similar length.[3] WAV files can be made smaller through compression. Compressed files are easier to transmit and take up less storage space. But to be used, they must be converted back into the original format. Today, recording studios continue to save music as WAV files.

It took several days for everyone to complete their recordings. Graham let Maya do the work, but he showed her how to mix the different recordings. Maya had to lower the volume on Benji's piano track and raise the volume on Kimi's vocals. By the time Maya finished mixing the song, she was happy with the results. She felt proud of all the new skills she'd gained. But she worried that she had asked too much of her cousins.

So she contacted Benji, who was a busy college student, to thank him for his time. He quickly texted her back and assured her that it had been no trouble. He had simply used his headphones to listen to the song on his laptop and then used his digital keyboard to record the piano part onto a USB drive. It took just a few minutes to upload the track and send it to Maya. Benji told Maya that if she wanted to make more music for their grandparents, he was in.

On the day of the anniversary party, everyone came to Maya and Graham's house. After dinner, the cousins gathered. Maya told their grandparents that they had a surprise. Graham pulled the song up on his phone and connected to a Bluetooth speaker to play it for everyone.

"That isn't the Temptations," said Grandpop as he listened to the song.

"Maya, is that you singing?" asked Grandma.

Maya's parents, aunts, and uncles were all surprised too. The cousins had surprised everyone with the song. "Maya, we didn't know you could sing like that," her mom said.

Maya quickly explained that the song was a team effort. Although it had been her idea, Graham and all her cousins had helped. Working with her cousins had been a lot of fun, and Maya was looking forward to recording more songs with them. It would be a shame to let her new skills go to waste.

THE HISTORY OF MUSIC

Music is an art form that often combines instrumental sounds and vocals. Sometimes people create music simply for the beauty of its sounds. Other times, people make music to express specific emotions, such as the joy of a celebration or the sorrow of mourning. Found in every society around the world, music is part of religious ceremonies and social gatherings.

Music is more than a soundtrack to human culture. It is a way of expressing and passing on that culture. This is because song lyrics may give information about what a group of people values or how the people see the world. As one generation after another learns the song, they learn these shared values. In some cultures, songs are also a way to pass down stories, ensuring that knowledge of a group's history or traditions survives.

Experts believe the first music made by humans was someone singing. No artifacts exist to prove this. But people who study ancient music say it is likely that a singer would have kept the beat by clapping their hands or beating stones or pieces

The Hurrian Hymn tablet contains two ancient languages, Hurrian and Akkadian. It is the oldest evidence of written music. The tablet is on display at the National Museum of Damascus in Syria.

of wood together. In 2008, Nicholas Conard of the University of Tübingen discovered flutes in a cave in southwestern Germany. One flute was made from a vulture's wing. The others were made from a swan's wing and from mammoth tusk, a material known as ivory. The flutes date back to approximately 35,000 to 40,000 years ago, making them the earliest musical instruments unearthed by archaeologists.

In the 1950s, French archaeologists excavated a palace in the ruins of Ugarit, an ancient city in what is now Syria. They discovered several tablets dating back to around the 1200s or 1300s BCE. Among them was the oldest evidence of written music, the Hurrian Hymn. It was written in cuneiform on a clay tablet approximately the size of a smartphone. The song is an ode to the moon goddess Nikkal. The tablet includes notations about where the musician's fingers should be positioned on the strings of the lyre while playing the song.

The Hurrian Hymn shows that ancient people wrote music so others could play it. But a standard way of writing music wasn't invented until 1025 CE. Religious music was written with symbols called neumes, which showed the singer whether the pitch should

ANCIENT INSTRUMENTS

A bull-roarer is a musical instrument that consists of an oblong piece of wood with a cord tied to it. The player holds onto the cord with one hand and whirls the instrument through the air in a circular motion. As it moves through the air, it makes a roaring sound that can be heard over long distances. The pitch is altered by twirling the instrument faster or slower. Bull-roarers have been used by Australia's aboriginal peoples, New Zealand's Māori people, and the ancient Greeks. Archaeologists have discovered several ancient bull-roarers.

slide up or down from the previous note. A monk named Guido of Arezzo noticed that younger singers struggled with this basic written music. This was because neumes only tell singers to sing higher or lower, not what the starting note of the song should be.

In approximately 1000 CE, Guido of Arezzo created the first musical staff system. This notation gave written music even more shape. During this time, music was usually written and copied by hand. Copying music was a slow process. This meant that copies of music were very limited in number. Most written music was owned by places such as churches and monasteries. At these places, people often sang during worship services.

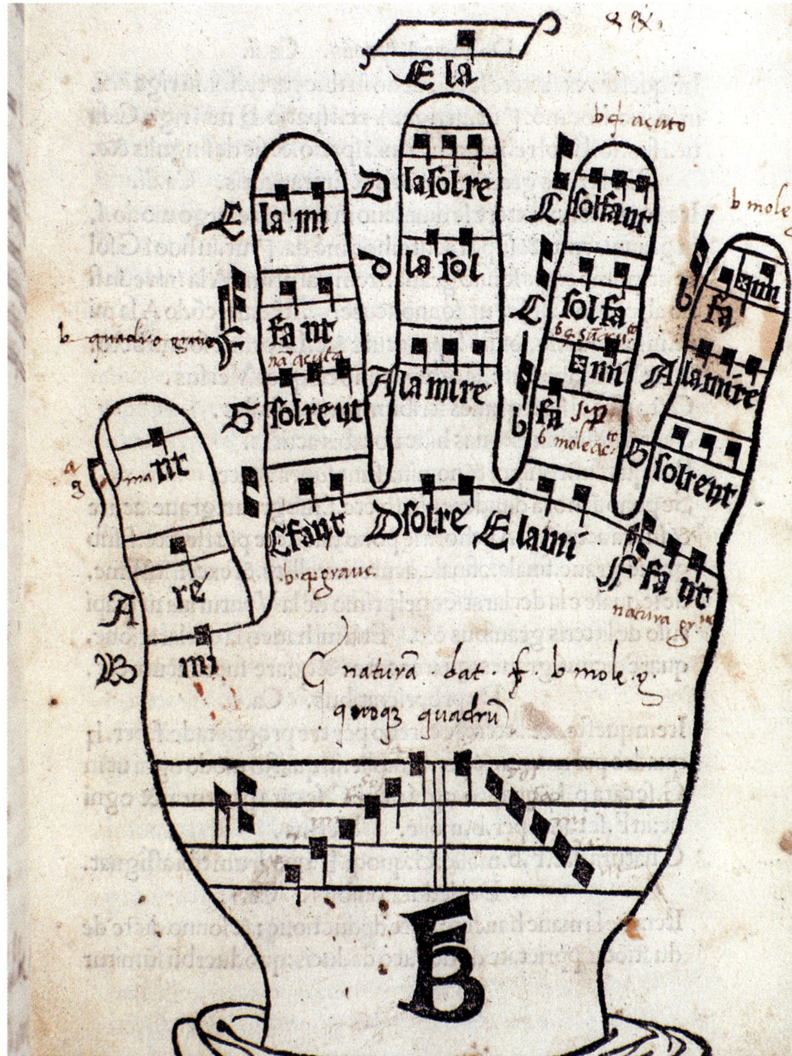

Guido of Arezzo's musical ideas were closely linked to the Guidonian hand, a medieval learning tool. It involved mapping out and memorizing music notes using the hand as a visual guide.

The earliest version of the Edison phonograph recorded audio on strips of tinfoil. Many new and improved models were released in the following years, such as the Edison Standard Phonograph in 1898.

FROM SHEET MUSIC TO EARLY RECORDINGS

The limited availability of music changed when the first machine-printed sheet music was created around 1470. This happened approximately 20 years after the invention of the European printing press. Machine-printed music was cheaper than hand-copied sheet music, and people could purchase and play music even if they had never heard the song played before.

Sheet music sold well for hundreds of years. Between 1910 and 1920, the sheet music for a hit song sometimes sold millions of copies. In 1910, one of the top-selling songs was "Let Me Call You Sweetheart." More than five million copies of sheet music for this song were sold.[1]

In 1877, American businessman and inventor Thomas Edison invented the phonograph. This device recorded sounds, such as talking or music, on wax cylinders. These sounds could then be played back. However, the sound quality of early phonograph recordings was poor. Edison did not follow up on the invention, and other inventors saw ways to improve it.

Emile Berliner, a German immigrant to the United States, patented the gramophone in 1887. It produced sound through a large brass horn and played flat discs that were easier to store than Edison's cylinders. The discs were made from shellac, a type of resin secreted by female lac insects, mixed with clay and other materials. These discs eventually became known as records. Between 1901 and 1920, most US homes had a record player of some kind. Some were decorative and expensive, but others were cheaply made and more affordable. The sales of records increased from four million in 1900 to almost 30 million in 1910.[2] Early record companies began to form in the late 1800s, such as the Victor Talking Machine Company. More companies formed throughout the 1920s.

Music became even easier to access when the radio was invented in 1901. It took until 1920 for the first commercial radio stations to appear in Wilkinsburg, Pennsylvania, and Detroit, Michigan. Home radios also became more affordable at this time. When radio stations began broadcasting music in 1920, record company executives worried about the new technology.

Records had only one song per side, which meant someone playing a record on a gramophone had to get up and replace the disc after every song.[3] In 1920, each disc cost around a dollar, which is equal to approximately $15.24 in 2023.[4] Meanwhile, someone listening to a radio could listen to endless music for free. Despite these concerns, most radio stations in the 1920s played very few records. They preferred to broadcast live music instead.

Facing competition from radio stations, record companies worked to improve their recordings. Many began using more advanced microphones to improve the sound quality of recordings. By 1927, Americans were buying 100 million records per year. But the Great Depression (1929–1939) ended this boom. During this economic downturn, people lost their jobs and struggled to feed their families. In 1930, the first vinyl records were created, providing even better sound quality. But by 1932, sales had dropped to only six million records per year.[5]

In 1948, the company Columbia Records discovered that the material polyvinyl chloride (PVC) could be used to make more durable vinyl records. Records made with PVC captured clearer sounds. Manufacturing vinyl records was also more efficient than making shellac records. In the 1950s, vinyl records became the primary format for recorded music.

From the 1970s through the 1990s, more innovations made music portable. Cassette tapes were plastic cases that contained magnetic tape on which music was recorded. Tapes could be played in devices called cassette players. Some cassette players were portable, such as the Sony Walkman. The Sony company developed this device in 1979.

Other cassette players were part of home stereo systems, cars, or portable stereo systems called boomboxes. With cassette tapes, people could record music they heard

PHONOGRAPH PARLORS

In 1889, the first phonograph parlor opened in San Francisco, California. By the 1890s, people could visit these parlors in most major cities. Each parlor contained numerous phonographs, and people would line up to take a seat and listen. When it was their turn, the customer would use a speaking tube to tell the operator which song or comedy piece they wanted to hear. Then they would put a tube in each ear to listen to the song. The customer would be billed for each song they listened to.

VICTOR RECORDS
COLUMBIA
DECCA
OKeh
Bluebird RECORDS
Continental
Decca
POLKAS
RHAPSODY IN BLUE
DECCA MODERN American MUSIC
THIS IS THE ARMY
WHITE CHRISTMAS
DEEP IN THE HEART OF TEXAS

on the radio and create mixtapes of their favorite songs. These shareable tapes functioned as early versions of playlists. People used them to share music with each other.

MUSIC GOES DIGITAL

In the 1970s, the companies Sony and Philips were both researching how to record music digitally on discs. The companies decided to work together. They created the first compact discs (CDs). Engineers at Philips figured out how to manufacture and encode the discs.

Meanwhile, Sony employees created digital error correction, a mathematical technique for correcting errors in digital data transmission. This made it possible to reliably play the data back. Smaller and easier to store than vinyl records, CDs could hold about 74 minutes of music.[6] They were also sturdier and less prone to breakage than records.

The first album released on CD was Billy Joel's *52nd Street*. It became available for sale on October 1, 1982. It debuted in Japan alongside Sony's CDP-101 CD player, which cost

In the 1950s, stores sold vinyl records from many major labels, including Columbia, RCA Victor, and Decca. Records were stored in paper or plastic dust sleeves.

NAPSTER

In June 1999, 19-year-old computer programmer Shawn Fanning founded a platform called Napster. It cataloged music files that people who were connected to its network had on their computers, and users could download songs directly from other users for free. "It was something that provided a better, more reliable and fun way for people to share music and see each other's music collection," Fanning said in 2019.[10] However, the band Metallica and several record labels sued Napster for making it possible for users to illegally share music. The company went bankrupt in 2002.

approximately $730.[7] This is equal to approximately $2,300 in 2023.[8] Most early CDs featured classical music.

But this changed in 1984 with the debut of the Sony Discman, a portable CD player. The Discman appealed to young fans of popular music. In 1985, *Brothers in Arms* by Dire Straits sold one million copies on CD.[9] CDs eventually replaced cassette tapes as the primary medium for music.

By the late 1990s, the internet was firmly established in American daily life. It made sharing information quicker and easier than ever before. It also had a major effect on the music industry. People used file-sharing programs such as Napster to download songs and albums without paying for them. Record companies were alarmed and took legal action against these programs.

The ease of illegal music downloads inspired companies to change the way they sold music. In 2003, Apple opened its iTunes Music Store. Users could buy albums or tracks to download on their computers, without having to go to a store and purchase a CD. They could build up a personal music library over time, putting together playlists of purchased music. By 2010, Apple had become the world's largest music vendor.

CREATOR **SPOTLIGHT**

BILLY JOEL

Singer-songwriter Billy Joel grew up in Long Island, New York, and began playing the piano at age four. His parents wanted him to be a classical musician, but Joel was drawn to British rock music and American soul music.

Joel's first album, *Cold Spring Harbor*, came out in 1971. It had been poorly produced by Family Productions. Joel regretted the exploitative contract he had with the label, but he didn't know what to do about it. He moved to Los Angeles, California, where he played in a piano bar under a fake name.

Eventually, a recording of Joel's work caught the attention of Columbia Records. The label bought out Joel's other contract. His first album with Columbia was *Piano Man* (1973). By the time his album *52nd Street* (1978) was released as a CD, it had already gone platinum. This meant it had sold more than one million copies in the United States. Joel also won a Grammy Award for Album of the Year.

During his career, Joel has won six Grammy Awards for his music. In 1999, he was inducted into the Rock & Roll Hall of Fame. He was named a Kennedy Center Honoree in 2013, and the following year, he received the Library of Congress Gershwin Prize for Popular Song.

Billy Joel's album *52nd Street* featured a mix of pop songs and ballads. It was his first album to reach Number 1 on the Billboard Top 200 charts.

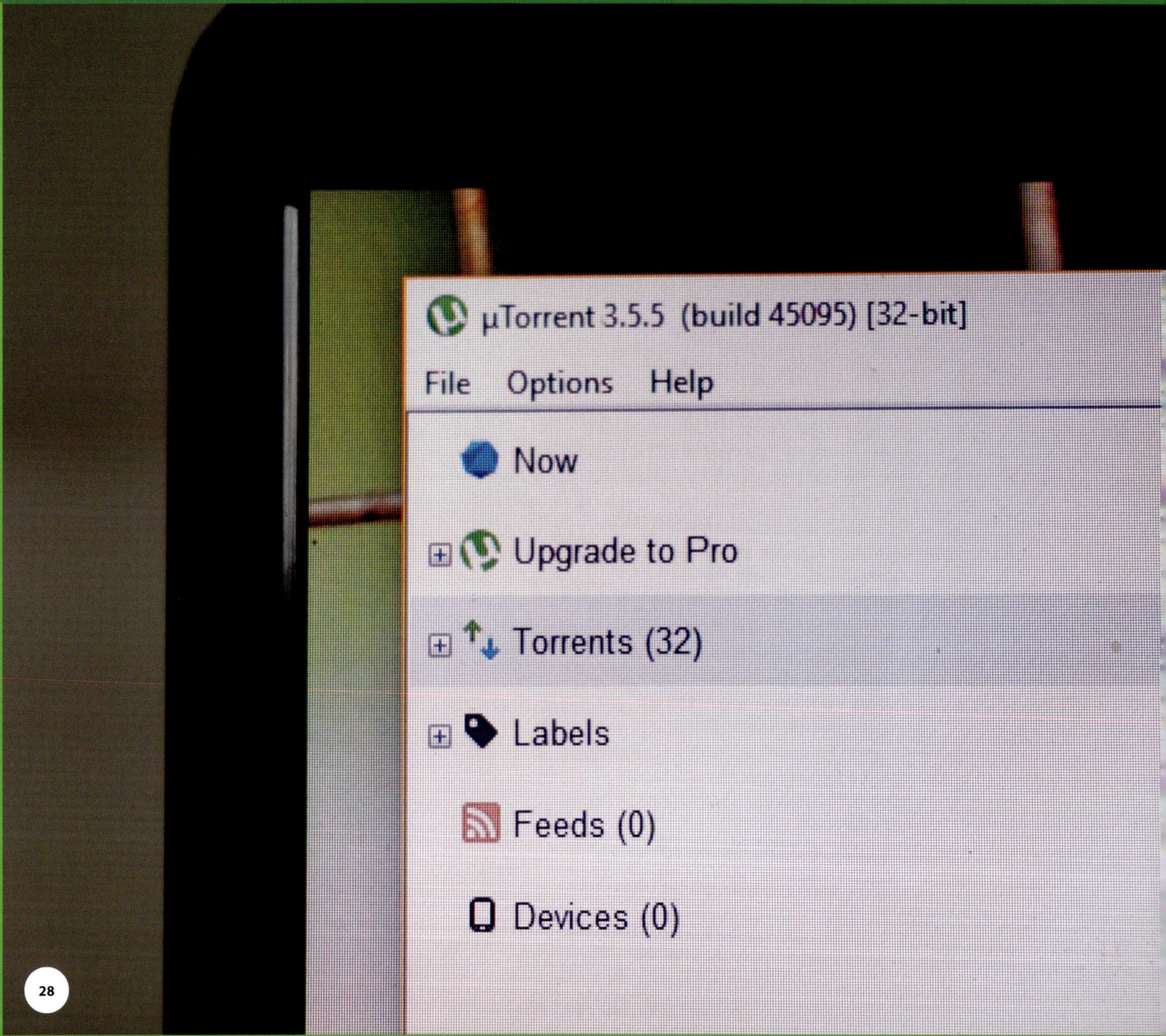
µTorrent 3.5.5 (build 45095) [32-bit]
File Options Help
Now
Upgrade to Pro
Torrents (32)
Labels
Feeds (0)
Devices (0)

Another shift in the music industry arrived in the 2010s with the rise of streaming services, such as Spotify and Apple Music. These platforms grew more and more popular in the 2020s. Rather than buying albums and songs, users can pay a monthly fee for unlimited access to a vast library of music. Artists are paid royalties each time their music is played on streaming services such as Spotify. How much money the artist earns depends on the agreement their label has with the streaming service.

In 2023, Spotify offered its 574 million users access to more than 100 million music tracks.[11] Streaming continues to drive the consumption of music. In 2022, the streaming music business in the United States brought in $13.3 billion. Digital music downloads brought in $495 million, while physical music purchases brought in $1.7 billion.[12]

> **"It's more of just thinking about the experience of listening to things on streaming platforms versus listening to individual CDs. You have to think about the way the consumer is going to receive the music more now. . . . The good side is, people are listening to more music than ever before.[13]"**
>
> ***—John Legend, singer-songwriter, on music streaming***

One early method of downloading music was torrenting. This allows users to quickly share or download files online. Torrent platforms include BitTorrent and Napster.

IN MEMORY OF TOM PETTY
LIAM GALLAGHER
AS YOU WERE
THE DEBUT ALBUM
FEATURING
'WALL OF GLASS' & 'FOR WHAT IT'S WORTH'
CD / DIGITAL / VINYL
OCTOBER 6
THE TIMES
STEREOPHONICS
SCREAM ABOVE THE SOUNDS
NEW ALBUM OUT 27TH OCTOBER

CHAPTER **THREE**

HOW MAJOR LABELS PRODUCE AND DISTRIBUTE MUSIC

Record labels are huge corporations that produce, distribute, and promote the music of the artists they represent. The three major US record companies are Warner Music Group, Sony Music Entertainment, and Universal Music Group. The biggest record labels are conglomerations, or parent companies, that own several labels. For example, Warner Music Group owns both Reprise Records and Atlantic Records.

Major labels are usually led by a chief executive officer (CEO) who oversees the entire company. A president oversees each label. There are often many departments within a record company. Each handles different parts of the process. The artists and repertoire (A&R) department finds new music artists to sign. It helps them select material for upcoming albums, chooses producers, and decides where albums will be recorded.

The art department is responsible for all the artwork needed to promote an album, such as advertisements and CD cover art. The legal department keeps track

Big record label companies often have multiple locations. Warner Music Group, for example, has more than 50 locations worldwide. One of the label's offices is located in London, England.

We help extraordinary talent cut through the background noise in our short-span attention economy, enabling them to truly connect with fans and . . . unlock a universe of opportunities.[2]

—Max Lousada, CEO, Recorded Music, Warner Music Group

of the company's contracts, including those signed by artists and business partners. It also handles any lawsuits involving the company. A lawsuit may happen between an artist and company if a contract's terms are not met.

Another important department is new media. This department helps artists create music videos and maintain an online presence, which helps attract fans and boost sales of the artist's music. The promotion department works to get artists' new songs played on the radio and on channels such as MTV. Meanwhile, the company's publicity department persuades magazines and newspapers to write articles about the company's artists. It also books artist appearances on radio and television shows.

In 2020, the International Federation of the Phonographic Industry reported that record labels regularly invest between $500,000 and $2 million for an artist to break into the industry.[1] This investment varies widely because labels will not spend as much on artists who aren't expected to be high earners. To determine if an artist will be successful, record companies review data about music genres and similar artists. Major record labels represent many well-known artists and bands. Universal Music Group represents Taylor Swift and Bad Bunny. Columbia Records represents Harry Styles.

A record label's publicity team often seeks out promotional opportunities for an artist, such as appearances on talk shows. In 2022, singer Harry Styles performed on the *Today* show to promote his album *Harry's House*.

FINDING ARTISTS AND RECORDING MUSIC

The first step for a record label is discovering new artists. This is the A&R department's job. Finding new talent means listening to demos that artists record to showcase their music. But A&R representatives don't limit themselves to demos. They also seek out artists to sign with the company. These representatives read music blogs, explore social media platforms, attend concerts, and check out streaming services to find trending independent artists. This helps them keep track of which new artists people are talking about.

When A&R representatives find an artist, they must persuade the artist to sign with the label. When an artist signs with a label, such as Columbia, it means that only Columbia can produce and distribute their music. Because major labels have money and connections, signing with one can help musicians reach more listeners. In addition, the label handles all marketing and publicity for the artist's music.

"We signed Sam [Ryder] because we could see he had star quality and that he'd built a connection with his audience, but then you add in the songwriting skill that became so evident early on, [and] we just thought, this is what we're in business to do: sign and develop artists like Sam.[3]"

—Nick Burgess, copresident, Parlophone, 2022

Music producers often supervise and guide artists during recording sessions in the studio. They may also help operate recording equipment.

ABBEY ROAD RECORDING STUDIO

The world's first recording studio, Abbey Road, was established in 1929. The Gramophone Company spent two years converting a house in London into the iconic studio. The studio officially opened in 1931 with three recording spaces of different sizes. Additional studios were added in 1980 and 2017. Artists who have recorded at Abbey Road over the last 90 years include the Beatles, Ella Fitzgerald, Florence and the Machine, Ed Sheeran, Kanye West, Lady Gaga, Amy Winehouse, and Adele.

But signing with a label also means the label owns the artist's recordings. The artist gets only a small portion of the profits generated through the sale of their music. Still, a small portion of a very large amount of money can be a solid income for artists who sign with labels. Once the contract has been signed, the artist can begin making an album with the assistance of the A&R department.

In the past, most major labels had in-house recording studios. Today, many still do. Universal Music Group owns two well-known studios: Abbey Road in London, England, and Capitol Studios in Los Angeles, California. A&R representatives schedule studio time for the artist, either at a company studio or at an independent recording studio. A&R brings in a producer to oversee the album's production. The producer, artist, and A&R representatives work together to select a concept or theme for the album. Then the artist writes the music, rehearses, and perfects it before recording it in the studio.

Professional recording studios are specially designed for playing and recording music. The main part of the studio is where the musician works. It has rooms set up with special technology and equipment. This space often has instruments, music stands,

Professional recording studios can be used by groups of all sizes, including solo artists, bands, and even orchestras. Many studios provide instruments and high-tech recording equipment for artists to use.

and microphones. Recording studios are typically soundproofed with materials such as foam wall panels. This ensures high-quality sound. Many studios have trained staff members, such as a studio manager and lead producer. The producer works closely with the musician as they record their music. Artists may record with headphones so they can hear themselves as they sing or play, consult the staff, or listen to tracks after recording.

Most professional recording studios also have a booth or control room in which audio technicians and editors operate a sound-mixing console. They use the console to adjust sound levels as the musician makes their recording. The control room also contains computers with digital audio workstation (DAW) software. A DAW is basic music production software that enables musicians to record, edit, and produce audio files on phones or computers.

A DAW allows users to adjust sound levels and combine separately recorded tracks. Recording at a professional studio can give musicians access to special equipment and experienced, knowledgeable staff. The team can help the musician create a polished, high-quality recording.

DIGITAL DISTRIBUTION AND DATA

In the past, record labels produced physical products such as vinyl records, cassette tapes, and CDs. Although music fans still purchase records and CDs, the focus has shifted to digital music distribution. In 2022, 3.4 trillion songs in the United States were available as on-demand audio streams.[4] During the first half of 2023, the income from streaming was $7 billion, which was 84 percent of all recorded music income.[5] Record labels receive this income, which is shared with artists, every time someone listens to a song on a streaming service.

Many artists release albums of music. Many also release singles, or one song at a time. By releasing a single, an artist can track the song's reception by fans and then release another song weeks or months later. The goal of this release pattern is to keep listeners engaged and eager for the artist's next music. Releasing one song at a time has changed the contracts that artists sign with labels. In the past, an artist would sign a contract stating that they would work on a certain number of albums with the label. Now, contracts are usually for a set time period during which a specific number of songs will be released.

Recording companies often base decisions on music analytics. This is the analysis of data that reveals how popular a song or artist is. In the past, record labels tracked a song's popularity by

TAYLOR'S VERSION

In 2018, singer-songwriter Taylor Swift left the label Big Machine Records to work with Universal Music Group's Republic Records. But in 2019, Big Machine Records was sold to a company led by music manager Scooter Braun. This meant Braun would have the rights to all of Swift's master recordings that had been made at Big Machine Records and that he could make money off Swift's music. In response, Swift made a contract with Republic Records that ensures she owns the rights to all future master recordings she makes. She also began rerecording and releasing new versions of her Big Machine Records albums, beginning with *Fearless (Taylor's Version)* in 2021. Swift owns the rights to these rerecorded songs. In 2023, Swift released her fourth rerecorded album, *1989 (Taylor's Version)*.

looking at factors such as record sales and how often the song played on the radio.

Today, streaming services such as Spotify gather information about which songs are streamed most often and by whom. These services gather listener data and demographics, including age, gender, and location. They also gather data about users' listening habits, such as which music genres a listener prefers, if they listen to the same artists repeatedly, and if they prefer new or old releases.

Labels may look at skip rates, or how often a song in a playlist is skipped over. They may also pay attention to which songs listeners add to playlists, which devices they use to listen to music, and which search terms helped listeners find a song.

By gathering this data, record labels can identify emerging music genres. This affects not only which new artists the label signs but also which songs are chosen for artists to record. Knowing who is listening to which types of music also influences marketing campaigns. It helps record labels know where they can reach people who will enjoy a particular song.

Professional artists often earn a large portion of their income from concert tours. Taylor Swift reportedly earned 85 percent of all revenue generated from her 2023 Eras Tour, an estimated amount of $4.1 billion.

This can influence the partnerships that producers seek for musicians.

MUSIC AND INFLUENCERS

One method of social media marketing is getting influencers to promote songs. To do this, an artist must look for influencers who post about music. The artist should look for people with lots of engagement. But the influencers' posts, values, and brands must also align with the artist's. That way, the influencers' followers are more likely to stream or purchase the artist's music. Once an artist finds influencers they want to work with, the artist contacts them and asks them to promote their song. Usually, these influencers are paid a fee for each post.

SOCIAL MEDIA AND GAMING

Many record labels use social media to market their musicians. They encourage artists to be active on social media platforms. There, they can interact with fans and get feedback on their work.

Interacting with the public helps musicians reach out to new listeners. Labels encourage artists to use platforms such as Facebook, Instagram, and YouTube. They may have them engage with fans on streaming platforms such as Amazon Music, Apple Music, and Spotify.

Labels may also organize social media events. Jenifer Mallory was an executive at Sony Music Entertainment. She said Sony reached out to YouTube influencers in Taiwan, Australia, and the United Kingdom who played ukuleles. Sony asked them to film themselves playing a song by Grace VanderWaal, one of Sony's artists. They used the influencers' videos to create a piece that demonstrated the song's global outreach.

Because social media is on-screen, visual storytelling is increasingly important when it comes to music marketing. This includes music videos, lyric videos, and behind-the-scenes videos. Being on-screen attracts attention to an artist and their music. Some labels, such as United Music Group, hire staff to create social media content and music videos.

Artists can also use video games to promote their music, appearing in games as playable characters or giving virtual concerts. In 2023, gaming company Activision added rap artists Nicki Minaj, Snoop Dogg, and 21 Savage to *Call of Duty: Modern Warfare II*. The artists even recorded lines of dialogue for the game. Players could purchase the characters for approximately $20 each and use them in multiplayer online battles.[6] This type of promotion allows artists to reach new audiences. The music website Complex looked at social media reactions to the news, noting, "Several people openly admitted they've never played the game but would go ahead and start since Nicki will be a part of it."[7]

Some artists have performed virtual concerts inside the world of the popular video game *Fortnite*. In 2021, pop singer Ariana Grande partnered with the battle royale game for its three-day Rift Tour. Millions of players tuned in to watch Grande perform her hit songs as an avatar. The event was unique because it blended aspects of the game with Grande's performance. Players journeyed into a portal that took them through a series of fantastical worlds. The singer described the concert as "an unforgettable, magical journey to new realities."[8] She reportedly made more than $20 million off the event, and it boosted the number of people streaming her songs.[9]

Because gaming companies earn so much money, some music industry leaders are reaching out and requesting partnerships. To do this effectively, labels must learn about individual games and find the right artist to match with the game. A game whose players see themselves as edgy or subversive won't be drawn to a commercial, mainstream artist. A game with a low-key, understated community may not accept an artist who is into shock and spectacle. One way for music and gaming to work together is for the artist to create original branded content for the game.

In 2020, rapper Travis Scott partnered with *Fortnite* for a virtual concert called Astronomical. More than 27 million players tuned in to the event.

FORTNITE
DELL

HOW INDIE ARTISTS MAKE MUSIC

An independent, or indie, artist is any musician who is not signed to a major label. Some indie artists work entirely on their own, while others sign with small independent labels. Independent record labels are not connected to any major labels or the smaller companies they own. In the past, an artist's success usually depended on their ability to sign with a major label and get their music played on the radio. Today, artists have more options for exposure. But making it as an indie artist still takes a lot of work.

When singer-songwriter Ed Sheeran moved to London in 2008, he couldn't afford a place to live and slept outside near Buckingham Palace. He made money by playing at small venues and by busking, or playing music in public for donations. In 2009, Sheeran recorded and released an EP, or extended-play recording. He also worked on developing his vocal skills, signing up for the Artist Development course at Access Creative College. Sheeran played more than 300 performances in one year.[1]

Since releasing the hit song "The A Team" in 2011, Ed Sheeran has released several successful studio albums and started his own record label, Gingerbread Man Records.

Sheeran forged connections with other musicians, and he was asked to accompany the musician Example on tour in 2010. That same year, Sheeran recorded and released the song "The A Team." In 2011, he performed the song on *Later . . . with Jools Holland*, a British television program showcasing new talent. The song sold 58,000 copies in a single week, landing on the top ten lists in eight different countries.[2] After eventually achieving success as an indie artist, Sheeran signed with Warner Music Group's Asylum/Atlantic Records in 2011.

> **"It's increasingly normal for independent artists to crack the top of the charts.[5]"**
>
> ***—Tatiana Cirisano, music industry analyst, 2022***

Sometimes an indie song becomes a big hit on its own. This happened in 2022, when singer-songwriter Lauren Spencer-Smith was in a recording session for her song "Fingers Crossed." She posted a casual 47-second video of the session on TikTok. The clip earned 23 million views, and the song went viral on TikTok. It was the Number 1 song on Spotify's Pop Rising playlist with more than 32 million streams.[3] "I definitely felt in order to do something like this, I needed a huge label behind me and I needed a machine of people in marketing with a budget," said Spencer-Smith. "But the fact is that we have not put a single dime behind marketing this song, and it's already doing what it's doing."[4]

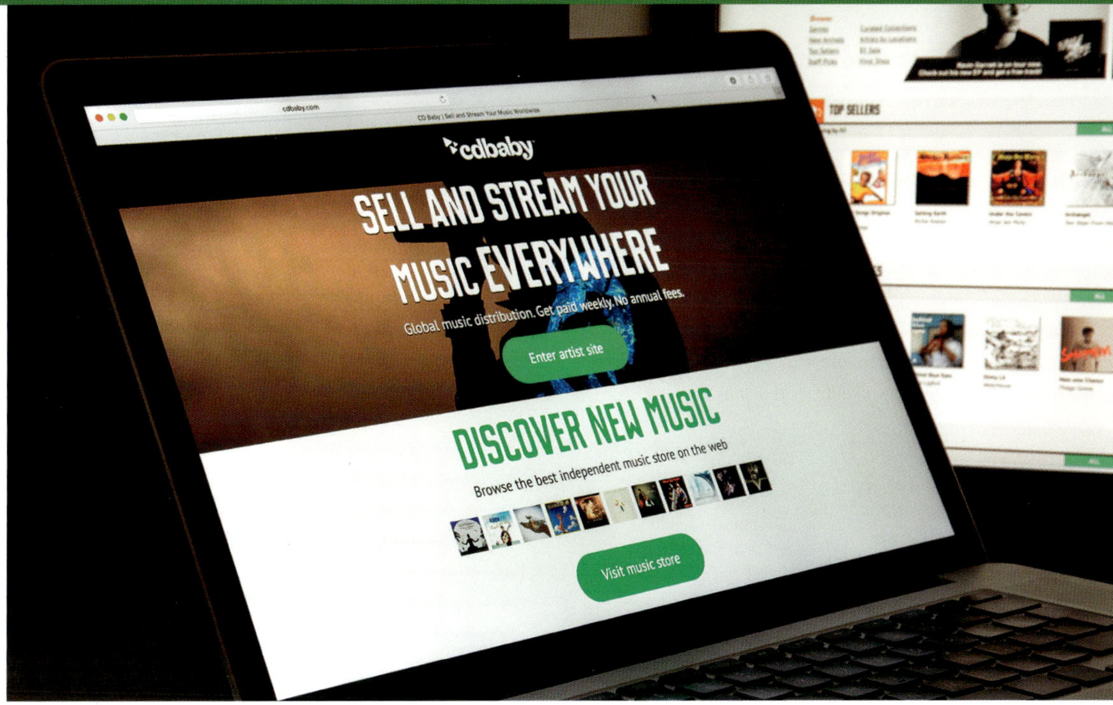

Indie artists who use the distribution service CD Baby have to pay a one-time fee each time they upload an album or single. The service has more than 150 distribution partners, including Spotify and YouTube.

There are three different types of independent artists. DIY, or do-it-yourself, artists have no recording contracts. They make all their own decisions and use online music distribution services such as TuneCore, Ditto, DistroKid, and CD Baby. For a fee, a distribution service uploads the artist's songs to major streaming platforms such as Spotify, YouTube, and iTunes.

Semi-independent artists pay label service companies, such as Awal, Absolute, and Believe, to provide the same services that a record label would, including marketing,

Indie record label Delicious Vinyl has represented many successful hip-hop artists. Its imprint Delicious Vinyl Island spotlights artists from the Caribbean, such as Jamaican artist Blvk H3ro.

distribution, and promotion. However, label services differ from major labels in that artists do not sign long-term contracts. Artists also pay for only the services they need and retain the copyrights to their music.

Other independent artists choose to sign with independent record labels. These companies are not connected to major labels and are privately funded. XL Recordings and Domino are two independent labels.

MAJOR PLATFORM PROGRAMS

Several social media platforms have launched programs to support new musical artists. TikTok's Elevate launched in 2023. It identified six rising artists: CHINCHILLA, Sam Barber, Omar Courtz, Isabel LaRosa, LU KALA, and Kaliii. TikTok invited each artist to share new content and updates on their work, along with insights about how TikTok has influenced their careers. The platform also planned performances in the artists' hometowns and home countries.

INDEPENDENT LABELS

Major labels are a vital part of the modern music industry, but artists do not have to partner with them to find success. Many independent labels also help artists achieve renown. In 2022, independent labels had taken control of approximately 43 percent of the total music market. This percentage amounted to almost $10 billion.[6]

One of the top independent labels is British company XL Recordings, which was founded in 1989. Unlike some other indie labels, XL Recordings works with a broad range of artists. But the company also has a knack for signing artists that go on to become global sensations. The label's most well-known artists are Adele and Radiohead.

Self-releasing artists and independent labels have an inherent advantage of being incredibly nimble.[7]

—Paul Pacifico, CEO, Association of Independent Music

Another top indie label is Seattle-based company Sub Pop Records, which was established in 1986. This label is known for fielding important indie-rock and grunge artists. Sub Pop was the first label to sign the rock band Nirvana. Another top indie label is Glassnote Records, founded in 2007. This company has signed several well-known artists, including Mumford & Sons and Childish Gambino.

Some independent labels have made a space for themselves in the music industry by specializing in specific music styles or genres. Major labels typically focus on music that will appeal to a global audience and bring in massive sales. But independent labels can choose types of music that will appeal to a smaller, specific fan base. For example, Ninja Tune specializes in experimental and electronic music. It has signed artists such as Bonobo, Amon Tobin, and Thundercat. The indie label Merge Records focuses on indie-rock and pop artists, including Arcade Fire and Neutral Milk Hotel.

In addition to signing niche artists who likely wouldn't find a home at a major label, indie labels offer artists greater creative control over their music and brands. Pop singer Nina Nesbitt felt her career had stagnated at major label Island Records. But her attempts to change her sound were met with resistance because the label had other female

In 2020, indie singer-songwriter Phoebe Bridgers launched her own indie record label, Saddest Factory Records.

pop singers. Island Records said that in order to fit into their list, Nesbitt should keep doing what she was already doing, even though it wasn't growing her fan base.

In 2016, Nesbitt signed with the independent label Cooking Vinyl. "Since going independent, I've just had a lot more control creatively," said Nesbitt. "The label I'm on are much more like, 'We'd rather you have a smaller fan base, but a loyal one. People that are actually into your music, instead of the ones who know a song off the radio but don't have a clue who you are.'" Nesbitt's career has advanced at Cooking Vinyl. In 2022, she had 4.6 million monthly Spotify listeners and made more money with each play than she had at Island Records. "I think it's concerning how small a slice of the pie people get on major labels," Nesbitt said.[8]

DISTROKID

Label service companies do more than distribute music to listeners. These businesses perform many of the same services as labels, including marketing, promotion, rights management, and data analytics. Artists who choose the label service DistroKid can select varying levels of service. Options include the Musician Plan, which costs $22.99 a year, and the Ultimate Plan, which costs $89.99 a year.[9] Different plans offer different services. Artists may be able to set up a landing page, where visitors can read about their work. They may also have access to a tool for building email lists, which can be used to send newsletters and updates to fans. Others allow fans to pre-add an artist's future songs to their Spotify lists.

MUSIC DISTRIBUTION SERVICES

When a fully independent artist records a song or EP, there are a limited number of places where they can upload their work online. Platforms such as SoundCloud and Bandcamp allow artists to upload their own music. Some online platforms do not allow artists to upload music because of problems with unstandardized metadata. Metadata is the identifying information that has been coded and embedded into music files. It includes the artist's name, songwriting credits, the song's release date, and genre tags. This metadata helps potential listeners search for and find specific songs. It also enables platforms to track the performance of individual songs.

Unstandardized or incorrect metadata can make a song or album hard to find. It can also keep an artist from getting credit and payment when their song is played. But correcting metadata problems can be difficult. It requires an understanding of the algorithms and computer applications that create metadata.

This means indie artists often need to pay a distribution service to get their music on major streaming sites. These sites are known as digital service providers (DSPs). Major DSPs include Spotify, Apple Music, Tidal, Pandora, Deezer, and Google Play Music. Distribution services may upload artists' music to social media sites such as Instagram, TikTok, and YouTube. When a distribution service posts the artists' work to social media, it can ensure that the music is released across all media at the same time.

Music distribution services also ensure that artists get royalties for their music. Royalties are the amounts of money that artists get paid every time someone streams their songs. But allocating these royalties is complex. Without a distribution service, it

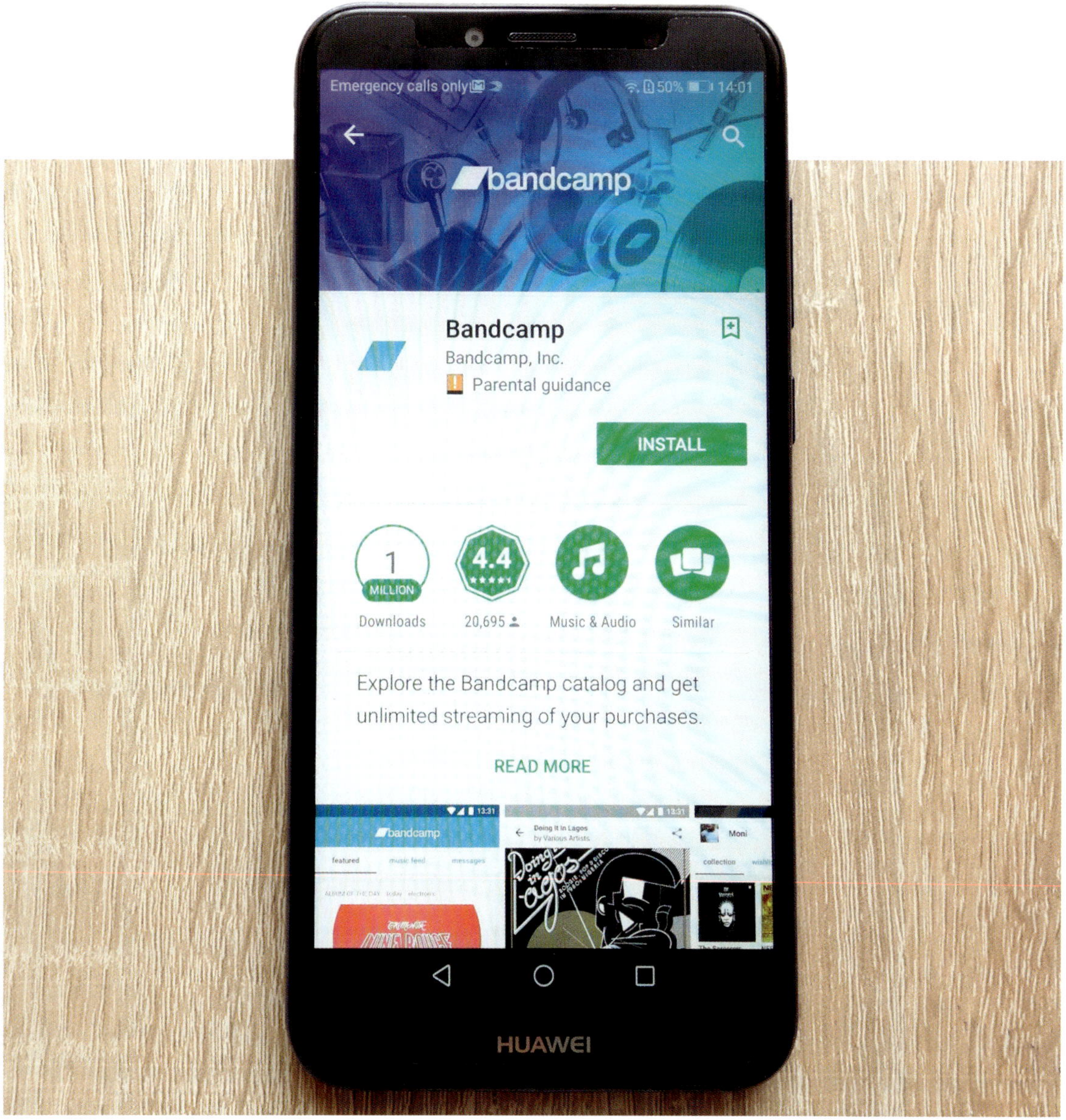

Some indie artists use a music distribution platform called Bandcamp. Users can stream songs and buy merchandise from artists.

would involve having every platform send a separate payment to each artist. The distribution service makes receiving royalty checks easier for an artist. The artist receives one check from the distribution service instead of a separate check from each platform. The distribution service makes sure artists are paid in a timely manner and receive the full amount they are owed.

RADIO

Some indie artists use the radio to market their work. Many people tune in to radio stations to hear their favorite DJs. People may enjoy a specific DJ's personality or music choices. Because of this, getting a song on the radio is similar to highly targeted marketing. Listeners are drawn to the types of music played by their favorite DJs and are likely to enjoy new selections as well. College and community radio stations are especially open to indie musicians. Most radio stations have information about sending in new songs on their websites.

CHALLENGES FOR INDIE ARTISTS

Independent artists face a wide variety of challenges depending on what type of artist they are. A DIY artist must take on every responsibility that comes with making, distributing, and advertising their work. Being a DIY artist is also a big financial responsibility. This is because the artist must finance everything that is normally paid for by a label, including promotions, tours, video production, and photo shoots.

In 2022, British indie rapper AJ Tracey told the BBC that some of his music videos cost more than $60,000 to make. "If I don't recoup on the video, there's no label behind me to write off that money. It's me," he said.[10] All expenses come out of Tracey's own bank account, and it is up to him to earn that money back. An artist who works with an independent label typically has some financial backing, but not at the same level as artists working with major labels.

Indie artists may also be responsible for marketing materials, such as videos and social media posts. When Nesbitt talked to the BBC in 2022, she was working on TikTok videos for an upcoming single. "There's definitely a lot more pressure on the artist to be the one that leads the creative side of things," she said. "It can be a bit overwhelming—so it really depends on what kind of artist you are, but for me it's worked really well."[11]

Not every indie artist feels this way, however. Some find the number of tasks required for their work overwhelming, especially the constant demands of social media. In 2022, music industry analyst Tatiana Cirisano told the BBC that independent artists must work to avoid exhaustion and burnout, especially since they are often made to feel like they need to continually produce content or risk losing their fans. "It's never been easier to release music independently, but the market has also never been so competitive," said Cirisano.[12]

There are many different reasons for an artist to choose an independent label, and these labels can help artists achieve local success. But this doesn't rule out the kind of global success that indie artists such as Ed Sheeran have achieved. After all, the choice of a label isn't permanent. Artists can sign with a different label if their circumstances change.

On TikTok, indie artists can participate in trends such as dances or lip-sync challenges. They can use their own music in these videos to expand their audience.

MAKING MUSIC AT HOME

People don't have to be professional musicians to record music. They don't need to rent a recording studio, either. Recording and mixing a song requires only a few key pieces of equipment. Affordable equipment options make it easier than ever for aspiring musicians to record music in their own homes.

The first thing someone needs is a place to record their music. A dedicated work area isn't essential, but it does provide a place to store equipment. It can also be a time-saver since the equipment does not need to be set up again each time it is used. A home studio setup can be as simple as a laptop, a microphone, a pair of headphones, and a table or desk.

Some type of computer or smartphone is essential. Many programs will run on either the Mac or Windows operating system. The computer should have enough hard drive space, memory, and processing power to store and process files. Most smartphones are powerful enough to run apps. Many people who are new to

Some musicians create their own home recording studios. A room such as a home office can double as a simple recording studio.

> **As long as you have space for a desk and a chair, you're basically ready to set up the foundation of your home studio.[1]**
>
> ***—Jon Foster, composer, producer, and drummer***

making and recording music choose to start this way.

A DAW is also essential for editing music. Musicians can use a DAW software program on their phones or computers. There are many different DAWs available, but new users often start with free programs such as Audacity, Ableton Live Lite, and GarageBand. GarageBand comes preinstalled on most Mac computers.

Musicians can use an audio interface to connect a microphone or musical instruments with digital outputs to a computer. The audio interface converts sound into digital files. This means it enables the sound picked up by a microphone to be stored digitally. It also processes the music played by a computer so that the sound can be played back through a set of speakers. An audio interface functions much like a sound mixer does.

In addition to a DAW, musicians who are recording at home may use a MIDI controller. This interface links to a DAW and can be used to control software sounds or virtual instruments.

APC40
Ableton
Arturia
MINIBRUTE

MICROPHONE OPTIONS

To know what microphone to buy, it is essential to understand what each type of microphone does. A condenser microphone is a fragile, expensive piece of equipment that easily captures even quiet sounds. A dynamic microphone may not capture the quietest sounds, but it won't pick up as much background noise as a condenser microphone. Background noise can be a problem in home studios since other people or pets may be in the home. A USB microphone can be plugged into a laptop and is easy to use. But many studio microphones have XLR connections. These are higher-quality but can only be plugged into an audio interface. An artist new to recording must make sure a microphone is compatible with the other equipment they plan to use.

Other essential pieces of gear are a microphone and headphones. A microphone is needed to record vocals or instruments that don't have an internal pickup or output. While recording, closed headphones work better than earbuds. This is because closed headphones generally deliver higher-quality sound. They also contain the sound so that it doesn't escape and get picked up by the microphone.

TIPS FOR A QUICK START

Someone who is new to music production has a lot to learn, but there are several simple tricks to keep beginners from feeling overwhelmed. Beginners can work with premade audio loops that come on a DAW. They can combine a music loop with drums or another percussion loop to create different energies and moods.

As beginners gain more skills, they can also combine additional loops to see what sounds work together. Basic loop sounds may include the keyboard, drums, bass, and melody. A more advanced set of loops might include the bassoon, organ, or xylophone.

DAVID BURKE (D4VD)

When self-taught musician David Burke, or d4vd, started making music, it wasn't because he wanted to be a musician. His plan was to be a professional gamer, and he needed noncopyrighted music to use as background music when he recorded himself playing *Fortnite*. Burke decided it would be easiest to make his own music. The Houston-based artist taught himself music and music production by using the social music platform BandLab, which he said was so straightforward he didn't even need to watch a YouTube tutorial.

When Burke started working on his song "Romantic Homicide," the song was happy and upbeat. But it wasn't working. After a few attempts, a lyric popped into his head, and suddenly it became a song about loss. By January 2023, "Romantic Homicide" had been played more than 807 million times on TikTok. It had been streamed more than 380 million times on Spotify and played more than 30 million times on YouTube.[2]

In the summer of 2022, Burke was invited to record in the studio with musician and producer Jim-E Stack, and he recorded three songs. Since then, Burke has continued recording music with BandLab. He says it is still his go-to way to create.

In 2023, d4vd performed at the Firenze Rocks Festival in Florence, Italy.

For beginners, it is best to start by keeping things simple. This might mean working with one drum loop and one bass loop instead of working with several of each. It is also best to limit the length of the song. Putting limits on early music creations gives new producers a better chance of creating something that sounds good. This will boost their confidence, leading them to try more complicated productions as they develop new skills.

Once a musician has used prerecorded loops to master the effects they want to achieve, they can create their own loops electronically. Instead of choosing a drum loop, they can select individual instruments such as kicks, basses, snares, and hi-hats to create a unique beat. Then, instead of choosing a music loop, they can choose their own electronic instrument, such as a piano. They can arrange notes to create different chord progressions and melodies.

Musicians who want more control over sounds and electronic effects can learn to synthesize, or create, sounds. Recording a sound is just the beginning. Once a sound has been recorded, it can be altered. For example, musicians can shift the recording's pitch or playback speed to create an entirely new sound.

SUPPLEMENTAL LEARNING

Using real instruments is another way people can produce music at home. Learning an instrument can help beginners learn more about music theory, or the study of the language and aspects of music. They will also learn to read sheet music.

Musician and music producer Mike Harwood recommends that aspiring music producers learn to play the piano. This is because the piano is a versatile instrument. Someone who learns the piano can learn to play many different types of music, including jazz, rock, and classical. Because of the wide range of notes on a piano keyboard, it is an excellent instrument for learning to create melodies, harmonies, and chords.

As someone learns to play the piano, they also gain a feel for which melodies and harmonies sound good together. These skills make it easier to produce music, giving musicians a better understanding of how to achieve the sounds they want. According to Harwood, beginners can learn the basics in a couple of months.

Some musicians may be interested in playing other instruments. The guitar is a good choice for people who want to produce rock, pop, folk, or blues music. Learning the drums can help musicians improve their sense of timing. Harwood's overall recommendation is that people who want to produce music should learn whichever instrument they are most interested in playing.

YOUSICIAN

People who want to learn how to sing or play instruments can use a variety of instructional platforms and apps. One of the leading platforms is Yousician, which has more than 20 million subscribers worldwide. Users can play or sing along to a variety of songs, including Metallica's "Enter Sandman." Users can also take advantage of more than 9,000 music lessons.[3] Reviewers compare the platform to the video game *Guitar Hero*, since music notes are mapped out on-screen and a microphone picks up the learner's playing and provides immediate feedback. In 2023, Yousician's basic package cost $14.99 per month.[4]

AUXY STUDIO APP

People who don't know how to play an instrument can use the app Auxy Studio to accompany their vocals. The focus of the app is on beats and electronic music. Users can select various options for drums and melody, which can include piano, bass, and acoustic guitar. Users can also learn to create chords and add bars of music to lengthen their audio loop. Some reviewers worry that because the app provides minimal directions, new users are likely to become frustrated and quit. But people can find tutorials and guides on YouTube.

Learning opportunities go beyond studying individual instruments. Young learners can take online music production courses. Some courses, such as those offered by McAllister Music Studio, are for specific age groups, such as teenagers. Other courses teach people how to use specific DAWs. Outschool, for example, offers GarageBand classes, while Udemy has courses on the music software Ableton Live.

Students can take college-level music production courses too, such as the ones offered by Berklee College of Music under Berklee Online. Some classes, such as those offered through Udemy, are free. But others, especially college-level courses, may cost more than $1,500.

COLLABORATION

Another aspect of music production is collaboration, or working with others. Sometimes collaborations are casual, involving musicians simply getting together to play music for fun. Formal collaborations may involve musicians working together on a specific project.

There are many reasons for musicians to collaborate. One is the fact that collaboration encourages creativity. When several musicians get together to work on a piece of music,

Learning an instrument can help musicians improve their sight-reading skills, or their ability to play a song they've never heard before by reading its sheet music.

each person has a different background. They may play different musical genres or have different training. As the musicians work together, encounter problems, or decide on the next steps, one musician is likely to come up with different solutions from another musician in the group. This can make a piece very different from what it would be if each musician was working alone.

By collaborating, musicians can learn to appreciate different music styles and techniques. They can also network with fellow musicians and artists. Working with other musicians enables artists to learn and grow together.

Alper Tuzcu is a composer, producer, and assistant professor at Berklee College of Music. One way he likes to collaborate is by cowriting songs with other musicians. "I find this process to be highly motivating, as you end up building confidence and trust in your process, as well as in your understanding of what works and what doesn't in a songwriting capacity," says Tuzcu.[5]

Some collaborating musicians meet in person, but sometimes class schedules and other responsibilities make

Many indie musicians collaborate on projects. In 2019, indie Irish singer Hozier, *right*, teamed up with country singer Maren Morris, *left*, to create a duet version of Morris's song "The Bones."

this challenging. Technology allows musicians to work together without being in the same space. They can even perform together remotely using videoconferencing apps such as Zoom, Google Meet, Skype, and FaceTime.

But musicians don't need to perform together to collaborate. Vocalists and musicians can record separate tracks on their own. Then someone acting as the producer can create a single piece of music out of those tracks. To do this, people must find a reliable way to share files, since the audio tracks are generally too large to send through email. One option is to use file-sharing and storage services such as Dropbox, Microsoft OneDrive, or Google Drive.

Indie musicians can collaborate by cowriting a song, arranging a duet, or remixing a song together.

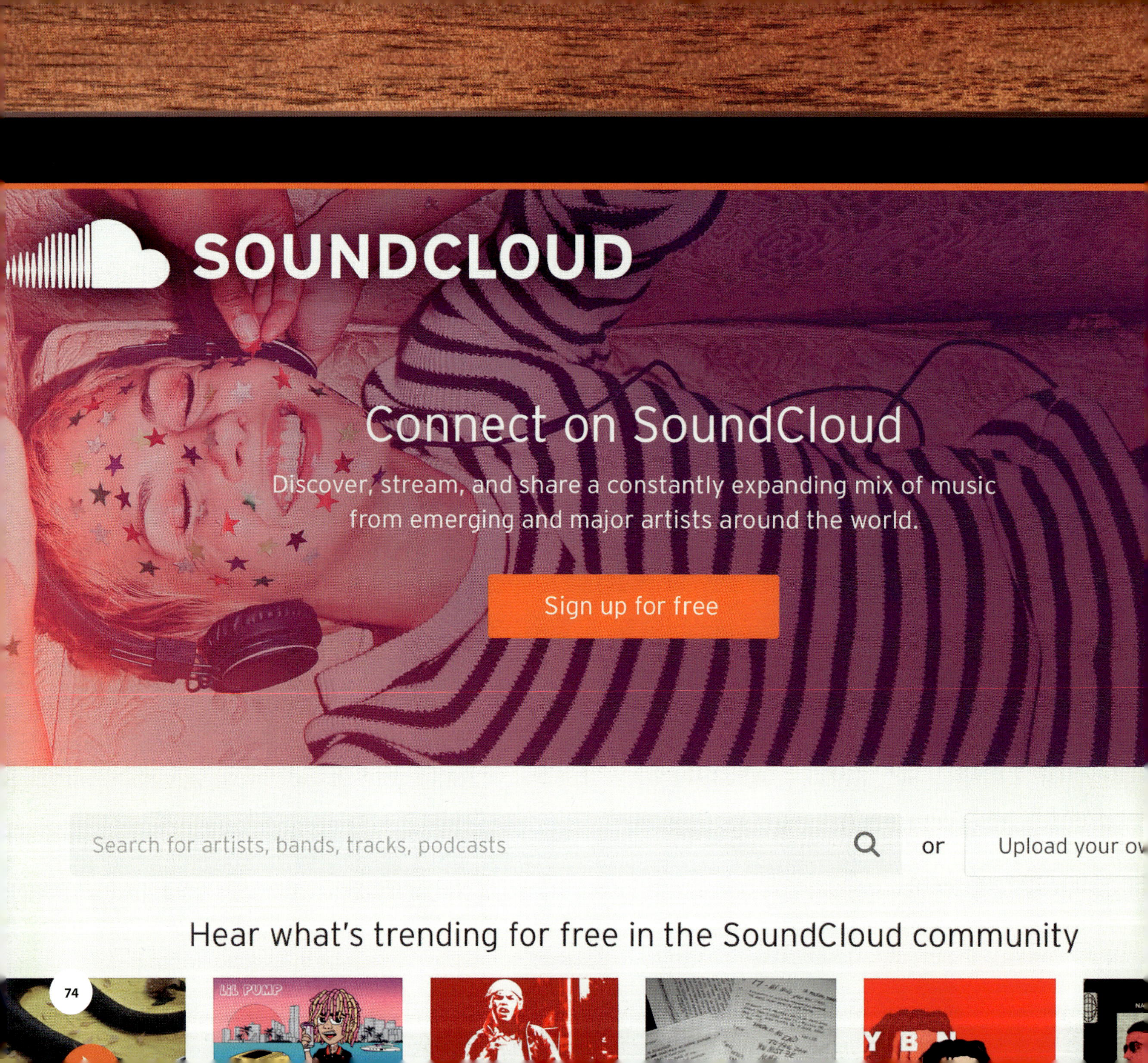
SOUNDCLOUD
Connect on SoundCloud
Discover, stream, and share a constantly expanding mix of music from emerging and major artists around the world.
Sign up for free
Search for artists, bands, tracks, podcasts
or
Upload your
Hear what's trending for free in the SoundCloud community
LIL PUMP

HOW INDIE ARTISTS DISTRIBUTE AND PROMOTE MUSIC

Making music is only part of an indie artist's life. Once an artist records music, they must get other people to listen to it. This means they need to share their music. Today, the exact amount of music uploaded online is a matter of some speculation. In September 2022, executives at Warner Music Group and Sony Music Entertainment told reporters that artists were releasing 100,000 songs a day. But others say artists are releasing half that amount.[1]

One streaming service that meets or exceeds 100,000 uploads a day is SoundCloud. From February 2022 through January 2023, an average of 123,000 tracks were added to the platform daily.[2] SoundCloud's numbers are higher than other streaming services because musicians can upload their own music to the platform instead of going through a music distribution service.

Whether 33,000 or 123,000 songs are uploaded daily on a platform, these numbers demonstrate just how hard it is for new musicians to break through. It isn't enough for an independent artist to get their music on a platform. They must

Artists who use SoundCloud can access promotional tools, engage with fans, and view listening reports for their music.

get their music to listeners. Sometimes, listeners share an artist's song on social media, helping it gain traction. This can make the song go viral.

ELEMENTS OF A VIRAL HIT

No one can be sure whether the song they are writing will go viral. But artists should still pay attention to the types of songs that do. No two viral songs are alike. "Old Town Road" by Lil Nas X and "Bad Habits" by Ed Sheeran are two very different songs that went viral. But one thing all viral songs share is that they connect deeply with listeners. They are songs that stick in people's heads. Most viral songs have a memorable melody and are quickly recognizable.

> **"The complexity of being able to separate one's music from the other 99,999 tracks uploaded that day is incredibly complex and incredibly difficult. Most creators don't have the capital, the skill levels, [or] the expertise to [promote] and be successful.[3]"**
>
> ***—Steve Cooper, former CEO, Warner Music Group***

Many viral songs have memorable lyrics. Sometimes these lines are funny or meaningful, but some are just catchy. One of these is the line "Hello, it's me," which opens Adele's song "Hello."

Many viral songs also stir specific emotions, such as joy or anger, that help grab the listener's attention. These types of hits are relatable too. Many focus on universal topics or feelings that many people have experienced, such as falling

In 2020, Lil Nas X won two Grammy Awards for his hit song "Old Town Road." One was for Best Music Video, and the other was for Best Pop Duo/Group Performance.

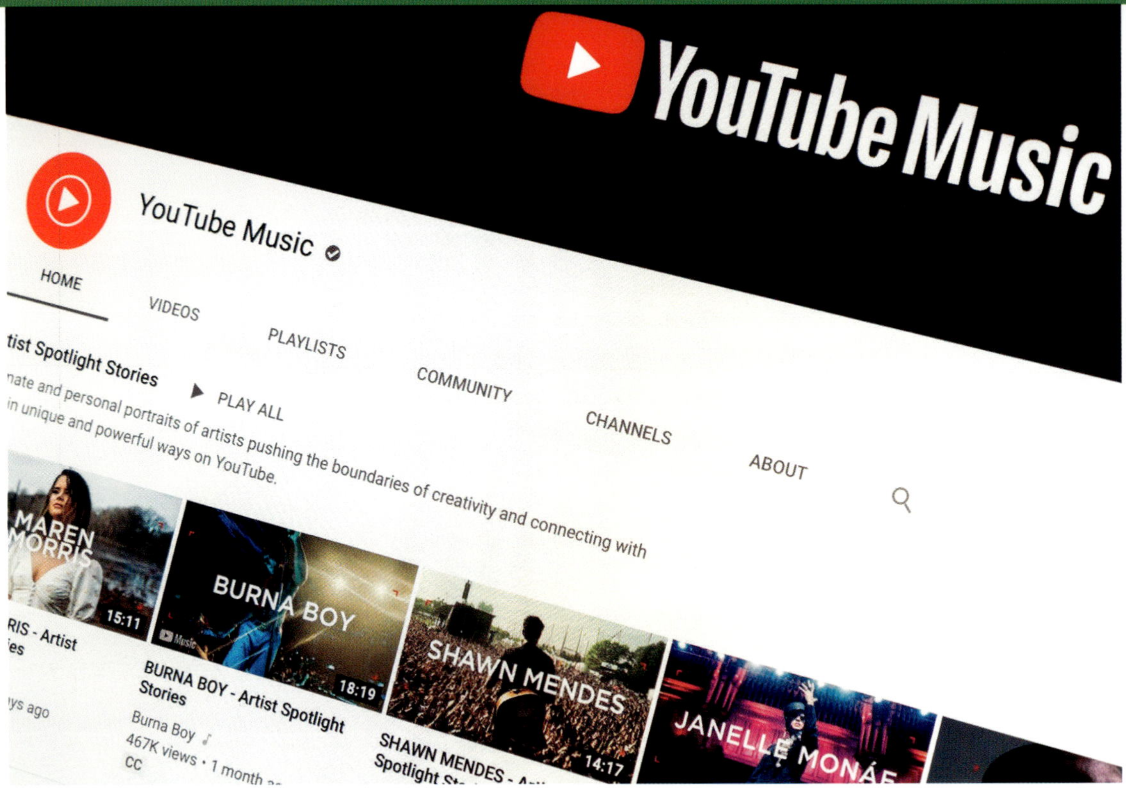

In addition to sharing music videos, artists can be featured on YouTube Music's Artist Spotlight Stories. In each video, an artist discusses their music.

in love or breaking up with someone. Other times, hit songs focus on loneliness, hope, or anger.

Sometimes quirky songs go viral simply because they grab the public's imagination. For example, Psy's hit song "Gangnam Style" brought K-pop to the attention of American audiences. It became known for the dance moves in its music video, which is one of the most viewed YouTube videos of all time, with nearly five billion views.[4] While a specific trait might make a song go viral, sometimes timing is also a factor. To achieve success, a song must launch at the right time, when listeners are hungry for whatever the song brings into the world.

SOCIAL MEDIA MATTERS

In addition to writing the best music possible, artists should make sure their work can be easily found on social media. The most important step creators can take is to get their work on various platforms. YouTube, for example, has helped advance the careers of artists such as Justin Bieber and Ed Sheeran. In 2023, *Entrepreneur* magazine reported that two billion unique users log on to YouTube every month.[5] And according to TikTok's website, the United States alone has more than 150 million people on the platform.[6] So it is no surprise that some artists, such as Lizzo, Doja Cat, and Bad Bunny, broke out because they found fans on the platform.

Finding fans requires more than just posting music online. TikTok's website offers advice for artists about how to make the most of the platform. One recommendation is to use two TikTok features, Duets and Stitch. Duets allows two videos to play simultaneously in a split-screen format. An artist can pick a video of another performer singing, tap on Duets, and record their own video accompaniment. The Stitch feature allows an artist to use a portion of another performer's video within their own video. TikTok also encourages

VIRAL CHALLENGES

Artists can promote themselves on social media by creating TikTok challenges. They should pay attention to what the latest challenges are. Dance challenges, for instance, are common. Group participation challenges can scale up quickly as each participant shares the video. But it is essential for the challenge to be unique and a good match for the artist's brand or personality. A musician may challenge people to do something while singing a popular song. Whatever the challenge is, it must be simple and safe for people to do.

artists to record videos in which they tell fans about how they became interested in music. This personalizes the musician and helps people connect to their music.

One of the best ways for creators to reach new fans is by frequently posting content. This is almost impossible to do with traditional music videos, which can take a long time and a lot of money to produce. For example, Metallica's music video for "Enter Sandman" is more than five minutes long. The Who's video for "Won't Get Fooled Again" runs nine minutes long. The length can be part of what makes traditional music videos expensive to film and produce. Music videos also require slick production, editing, and large casts.

In addition, music videos aren't the most popular form of online content. Today, more fans click on short-form videos than long-form videos. In early 2023, Google revealed that YouTube Shorts had 50 billion views a day.[7] YouTube Shorts is a section of the YouTube platform devoted entirely to short-form videos. In recent years, the short-form video format has exploded in popularity. For artists, this is good news because short videos don't take as long as music videos to create.

CHANCE THE RAPPER

One artist who has never signed with a label is Chance the Rapper, born Chancelor Johnathan Bennett in 1993. His first three releases were the mixtapes *10 Day*, *Acid Rap*, and *Coloring Book*. He surprised the music industry when he won three Grammy Awards in 2017. He took home the awards for Best New Artist, Best Rap Performance, and Best Rap Album for *Coloring Book*. It was the first streaming-only album to win a Grammy.

The business magazine *Forbes* reported that Chance the Rapper made $33 million in 2017.[8] This was partially because he played at festivals and arenas but also because he partnered with brands such as Apple and KitKat.

In 2019, Chance the Rapper released *The Big Day*, his first studio album. Numerous artists contributed to the album, including Nicki Minaj, Death Cab for Cutie, Randy Newman, CocoRosie, and actor John Witherspoon. The album debuted at Number 2 on the *Billboard* charts.

Chance the Rapper has continued to collaborate with other artists. In 2020, he released the single "Found You" with Ludacris. In 2022, he released "Wraith" with Vic Mensa and Smoko Ono. Chance the Rapper has shown that an indie artist with no physical albums can have a successful, award-winning career.

In 2023, Chance the Rapper performed for the *Today* show's Citi Concert Series in New York City.

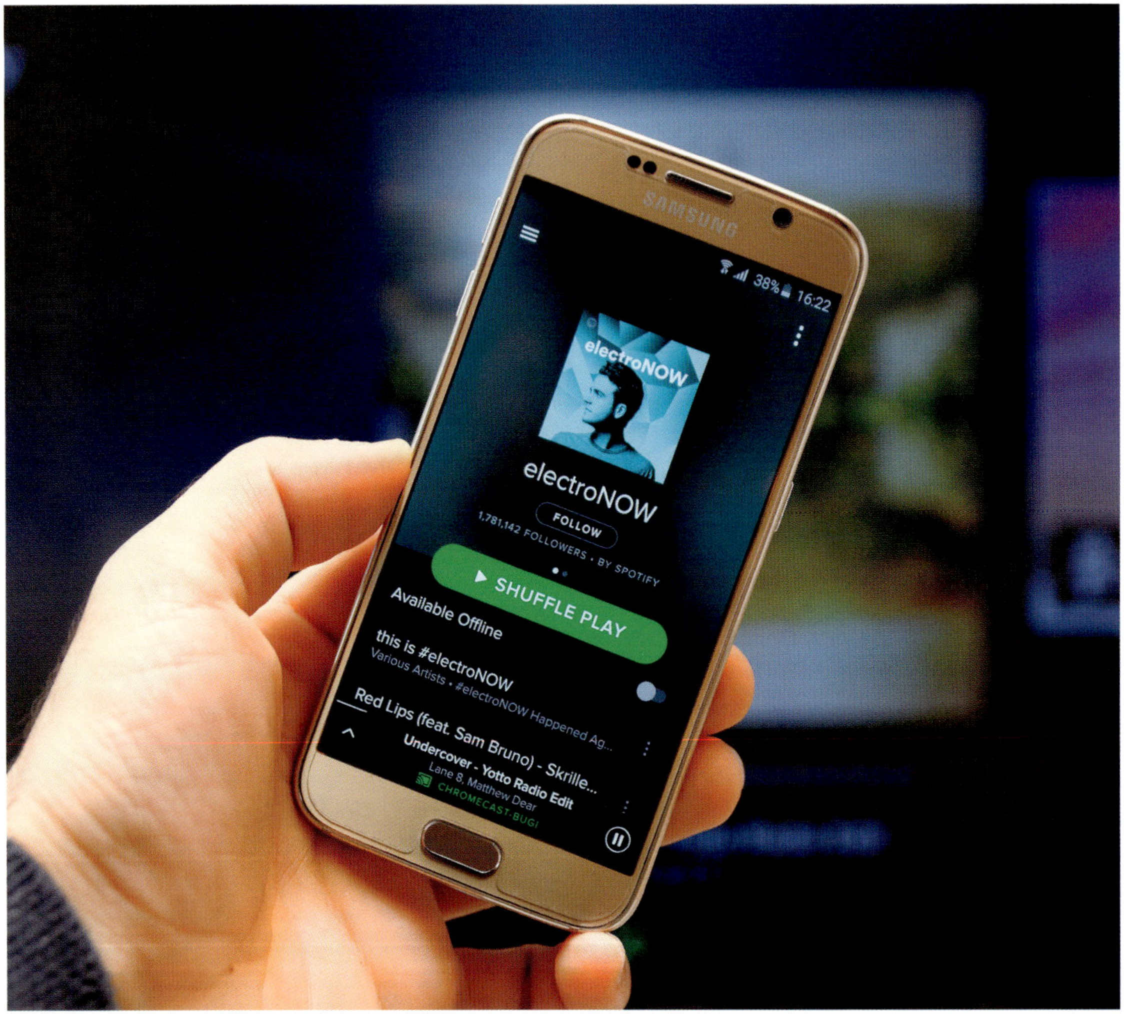

On Spotify, both artists and listeners can create playlists that organize music based on specific preferences.

Short videos can take a wide variety of forms. While working on a longer, more traditional music video, an artist could record a brief clip using their smartphone. Other possibilities for short-form videos include skits, dance numbers, a clip from a cover song, or a tutorial. These clips often have a raw, authentic feel that fans may appreciate more than a polished production. Many short-form videos are only about 30 to 60 seconds long.[9]

PLAYLISTS

Indie artists can also get their music in front of fans by adding it to curated playlists on platforms such as Spotify, Deezer, and Apple Music. If someone who sees the playlist clicks on the musician's name and listens to their music, they might become a fan. Even if they don't, the click improves the musician's statistics, as do follows, likes, and shares on the platform. Being on a playlist is also a great way for an artist to build their brand. Professional musicians often appear on playlists, so appearing on a playlist can make indie artists look more professional.

To get their music on a specific playlist, a musician must first contact the owner of the playlist. On Spotify, the easiest way to find the owner of a playlist is to read the playlist's

MAKING PLAYLISTS

Artists who want people to share their work can create their own playlists. If the artist includes works by popular musicians in their playlist, listeners are more likely to find the playlist while searching for those musicians. These people will then see and possibly check out music by new artists. One way to draw attention to a playlist is to curate one that fits a particular mood or theme.

"About" section. The musician should also look at other artists included on the list. If the musician is a rapper, it may not make sense to contact the owner of a playlist that features only electronic music.

Artists should look for playlists that match the genre or style of their music. When contacting the playlist owner, the musician should be professional and focus on making a good impression. Most playlist owners don't want to receive attached files, so the artist should include a link to their music to make it easy for the playlist owner to find.

A wide variety of people curate playlists, including influencers. It can be tempting to approach only big-name influencers about their playlists, but starting small can pay off. A playlist owner who isn't an influencer will likely be approached by musicians less often. Because of this, they might be more inclined to help an aspiring artist.

If an artist is added to a playlist, they should share the playlist on all their social media profiles. They should also remember to thank the playlist owner. This helps the playlist owner get more exposure. It is a good way to repay the owner for their efforts to promote the artist.

Apple Music users curate a wide variety of playlists. Listeners can find many playlists dedicated to indie music or emerging artists.

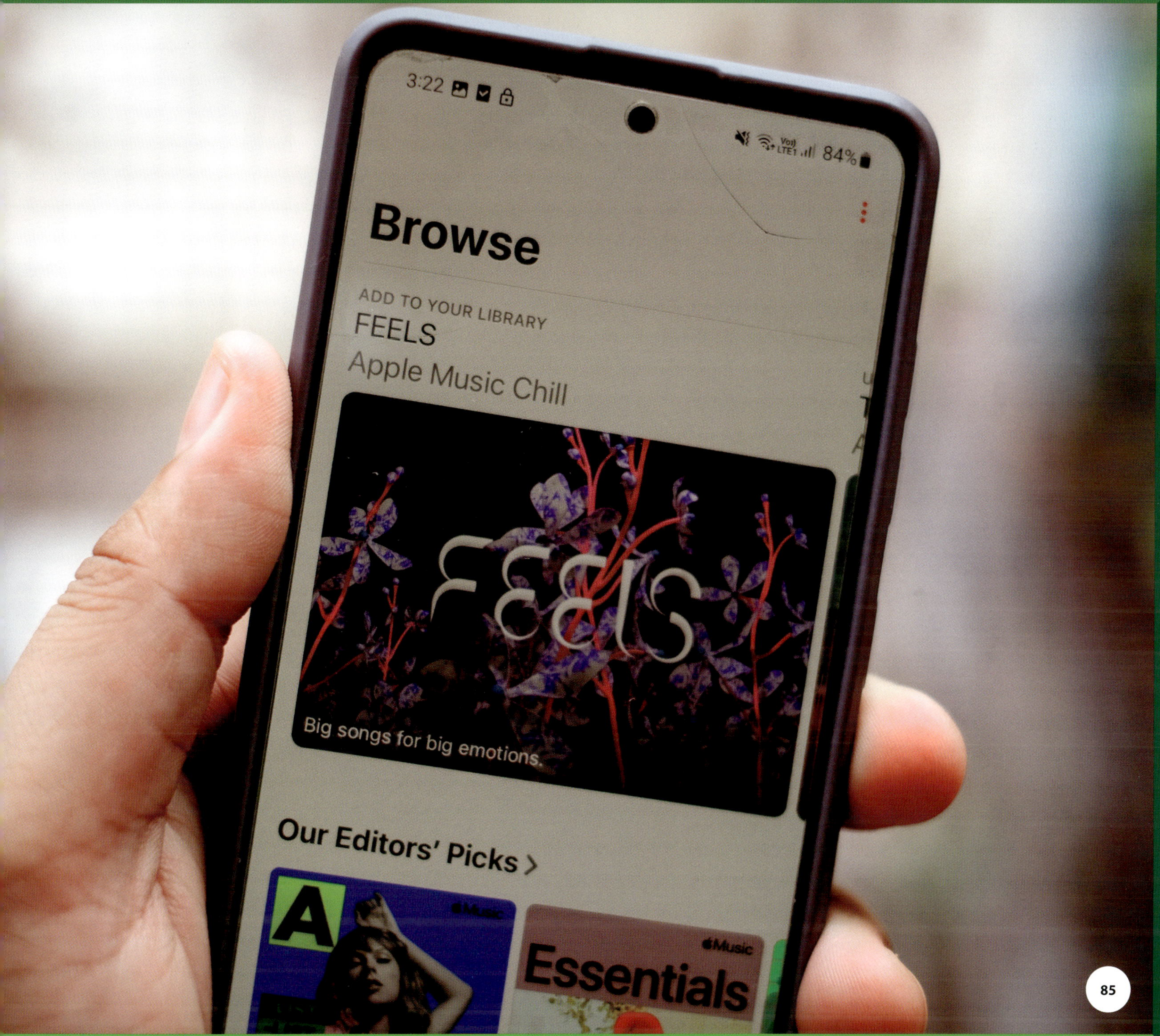
3:22
84%
Browse
ADD TO YOUR LIBRARY
FEELS
Apple Music Chill
FEELS
Big songs for big emotions.
Our Editors' Picks
Music
Essentials

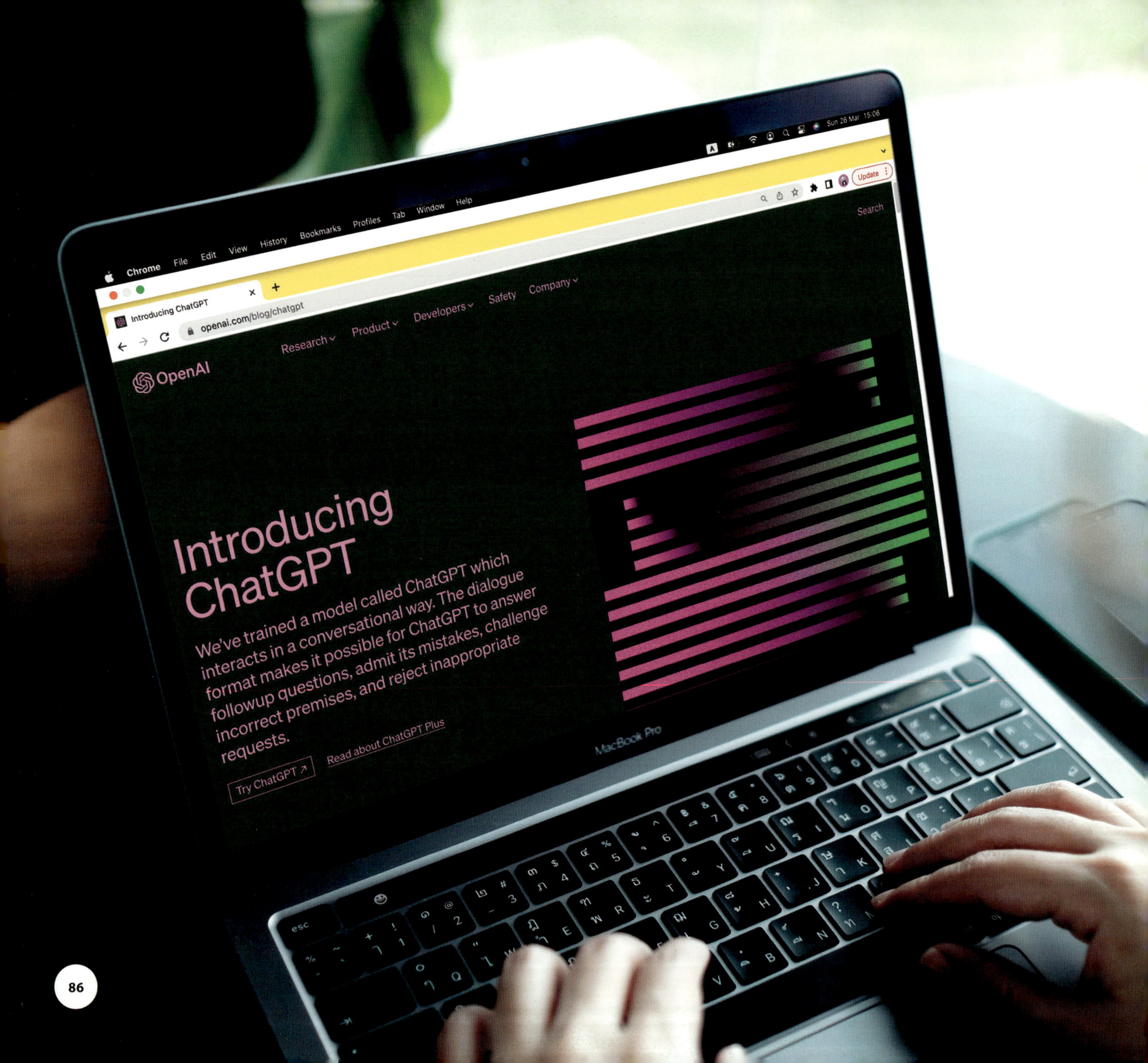

Chrome File Edit View History Bookmarks Profiles Tab Window Help
Introducing ChatGPT
openai.com/blog/chatgpt
OpenAI
Research Product Developers Safety Company
Search
Introducing ChatGPT
We've trained a model called ChatGPT which interacts in a conversational way. The dialogue format makes it possible for ChatGPT to answer followup questions, admit its mistakes, challenge incorrect premises, and reject inappropriate requests.
Try ChatGPT ↗
Read about ChatGPT Plus
MacBook Pro

CHAPTER **SEVEN**

THE FUTURE OF MUSIC

The digital world has become increasingly important to the music industry. Because of this, many of the changes predicted for the future of music involve computing. Many people believe some of these changes will come about because of artificial intelligence (AI). Generative AI programs are able to create various types of creative work, including text, images, and music. This type of AI has been around since 2014. But as the technology advanced in the 2020s, more and more people in creative fields began worrying about its potential effects.

AI AND MUSIC

In April 2023, Universal Music Group filed a takedown notice against the YouTuber Grandayy, who had posted a viral cat rap video. The YouTuber had used a voice duplication of the artist Eminem. It had been created using Prime AI, software made by the company ElevenLabs. This voice- and speech-cloning software was designed to re-create realistic human speech, avoiding the robotic sound of many

AI software such as ChatGPT could be used to generate song lyrics, compose music in a specific genre or style, or create melodies. But many people worry that the software could make it easier to plagiarize artists' music.

AI IN CONCERT

In 2022, David Dolan played a concert alongside AI at Stockholm University of the Arts in Sweden. Dolan played piano while a microphone picked up the sound. An AI computer system, created by Kingston University researcher Oded Ben-Tal, analyzed the sounds for data on pitch and rhythm. Then it improvised a musical accompaniment. "Creativity is not a unified thing. It includes a lot of different aspects," said Ben-Tal. "It includes inspiration and innovation and craft and technique and graft. And there is no reason why computers cannot be involved in that situation in a way that is helpful."[1]

synthesized voices. It can clone a person's voice or create an entirely new voice. The software is typically used to create audiobooks or dialogue for characters in video games. But the YouTuber had used it to duplicate Eminem.

The same year, the band AllttA recorded a track called "Savages." One band member, Mr. J. Medeiros, wrote the lyrics. Fellow band member Sylvain Richard, known as 20syl, created the beat. But then the band added an AI filter to the track. The filter created vocals mimicking the voice of rapper Jay-Z. Various rappers and entertainers commented on the YouTube post of the song, but it also drew the attention of legal professionals.

Attorney Ruth Carter works for the Arizona-based law firm Venjuris. She told Andre Lamar of the *Delaware News Journal* that AllttA's use of a synthesized voice doesn't break Jay-Z's copyright because a person cannot copyright their own voice. But if someone earns money by using another person's voice without permission, they could be breaking state laws that ban making money off someone without their consent.

In 2019, a team of experts began training an AI model on composer Ludwig Van Beethoven's works. Using Beethoven's sketches and drafts, they created a symphonic piece in his style. The Beethoven Orchestra Bonn performed the new piece in 2021.

AI technology may also change how songs are written in the future. Instead of collaborating with fellow human musicians, artists could use AI to help write lyrics or craft melodies and beats. AI could comb through vast databases of existing music to assist with production. For example, it might find a variation to a melody, help a songwriter avoid an overused chord progression, or find a better rhyme for a word. Many artists worry about these AI capabilities. They fear that AI could potentially copy their work, create competition in the industry, or even take the place of human musicians.

Someday, AI may be able to make music with little human intervention. Products such as Google's MusicLM are moving in this direction. While it isn't the first AI technology used to generate music, MusicLM can create more complex music than earlier systems.

MusicLM was trained on a database of 280,000 hours of music to learn how to generate songs in response to written descriptions, such as "the main track for an arcade game" or "British pop with innovative guitar."[2] If given a series of descriptions, it can create a piece that transitions from one segment to the next and lasts for several minutes. In addition, MusicLM can build on music samples ranging from a person humming a melody to notes played on a musical instrument.

"I think we'll have AI-powered styles and approaches to music which could be great to enjoy as long as it's done in a fair way, in a lawful way, and in an ethical way.[3]"

—Nick Eziefula, musician and lawyer, 2023

Musicians don't need to immediately worry about competition from MusicLM, however. The results of the technology aren't perfect, and sometimes the songs play more like fragments from several songs than one cohesive piece. In addition, the lyrics created by the program are only occasionally understandable. Other times, they sound like language but are actually gibberish.

Google has not released MusicLM to the public, but the program's creators aren't worried about the quality of the work produced. Instead, they are concerned about potential lawsuits. In experiments, they discovered that approximately 1 percent of the music created by MusicLM was not original. It had been copied directly from one of the musical samples used to train the program.[4]

VIRTUAL EXPERIENCES

Not all predicted changes in the world of music are controversial. The online world is creating new opportunities for the music industry. This includes virtual concerts, which allow artists to perform in front of much larger audiences than could ever fit into a physical concert venue. These experiences take advantage of the interactivity that is possible online, with some concerts even happening inside online video games. They take place in what is sometimes known as the metaverse, the collected universe of online communities.

Ariana Grande's 2021 *Fortnite* concerts brought together a total of 78 million fans over several days.[5] A concert of this size would be completely impossible anywhere else except in

AI VOICE CLONING

AI technology has caused controversy in the world of music. In 2023, an anonymous TikTok songwriter called ghostwriter977 released the song "Heart on My Sleeve." In the song, ghostwriter977 used AI technology to clone the voices of two popular musicians, Drake and the Weeknd. The song went viral on multiple platforms, getting 275,000 views on YouTube and 600,000 plays on Spotify.[6] But it sparked debate over the ethics of using AI to mimic other artists' voices. Universal Music Group, the record label that represents both Drake and the Weeknd, took legal action to get the song taken down from music-streaming platforms.

CREATOR **SPOTLIGHT**

DAMON ALBARN

The idea of a virtual band is not new. British musician Damon Albarn first found fame in the rock band Blur. But he came to believe that the music industry valued image over talent. In the 1990s, he and comic book artist Jamie Hewlett developed the idea for Gorillaz, an animated rock band. Real musicians were behind the group's songs. But in public-facing media such as interviews and music videos, the band members were depicted as fictional animated characters.

The band's self-titled debut album dropped in 2001. Its electronic sound combined elements of pop, hip-hop, and reggae music. People noted its influence in the next Blur album, *Think Tank*, which debuted in 2003. Albarn continued creating music in collaboration with other artists for Gorillaz and Blur. *Demon Days* by Gorillaz debuted in 2005. It outsold *Think Tank*, demonstrating the appeal of the virtual band.

In a 2001 interview, Albarn spoke about the band's success, saying he hoped to open doors for new kinds of virtual bands. "I think in a few years' time this will be the norm, so we just tried to set a blueprint that was of sufficient quality," Albarn said. "Kids are gonna be not only making music on computers, but they're gonna be creating amazing sorts of crazy images to go with that. And that will eventually mutate into a whole new kind of band, and hopefully, a whole new form of entertainment."[7]

In 2023, Albarn performed with Gorillaz at the Coachella Valley Music and Arts Festival in California.

the metaverse. Other artists, such as rapper Travis Scott and electronic DJ Marshmello, have also performed large-scale concerts within *Fortnite*.

Fortnite isn't the only game world that has hosted concerts. In 2021, YouTube hosted ESCAPE2021, an interactive live stream event. During the live stream, members of the South Korean band BTS performed two of their hits, "Butter" and "Permission to Dance," in the world of the video game *Minecraft*. Boxy figures representing the seven band members danced in unison and sang to an audience of virtual fans.

In the future, more artists will likely adopt avatars so they can perform virtually for an expanded fan base. Virtual concerts eliminate the need for artists and concertgoers to travel. They also allow for venues and experiences that could not exist in the real world. These metaverse events have become so vital to the music world that the MTV Video Music Awards launched an award for Best Metaverse Performance in 2022. The K-pop band Blackpink won the award. Blackpink's virtual performance took place in the world of *PUBG: Battlegrounds*, a battle royale game for consoles, PCs, and smartphones. The combat-free performance included choreographed virtual dances. The band members appeared as virtual avatars in a variety of landscapes.

Virtual artists have also made appearances in the physical world. The ABBA Voyage concert series features digital avatars, called ABBAtars, that represent the four members of ABBA. This is a popular band from the 1970s. The avatars perform onstage

HATSUNE MIKU

Hatsune Miku is a Vocaloid, an avatar for the Vocaloid voice-synthesizing software developed by Crypton Future Media. One of the first Vocaloids, Meiko, was released in 2004. For approximately $170, anyone with a computer could write a song to be sung by the Vocaloid voice. In 2007, Crypton released Hatsune Miku, who was designed to appeal to anime fans. The avatar had a voice bank recorded by sampling the voice of anime actress Saki Fujita. A record 40,000 copies of the avatar were sold that year. Since then, the Vocaloid has performed as a hologram projected on-screen. Miku even opened for Lady Gaga in 2014.[10]

as holograms with a live band and backup singers. The show opened in May 2022 in a specially built London arena. It sold more than one million tickets. Mark Sutherland wrote about the show for the entertainment magazine *Variety*. He said that at first, the holograms looked a little jerky. But as he watched the show, he could forget they were the creation of 160 motion capture cameras and one billion computing hours and just enjoy the show.[8]

But it isn't just avatars of stars in their prime that will perform in future concerts. Completely virtual avatar musicians and bands will perform in both the metaverse and the physical world. These virtual stars are created by teams of programmers who work behind the scenes. But fans can interact directly with the virtual stars on social media.

Hatsune Miku and Polar are examples of these types of artists. Within five months of launching, Polar had gained one million TikTok followers and 300,000 YouTube subscribers.[9] Now, these virtual artists perform music written by human creators. But improvements in AI will likely mean that eventually, virtual artists could perform or create AI-generated music.

The ABBA Voyage concert features songs from the group's 2021 album *Voyage*. The holograms are designed to look like younger versions of the ABBA members.

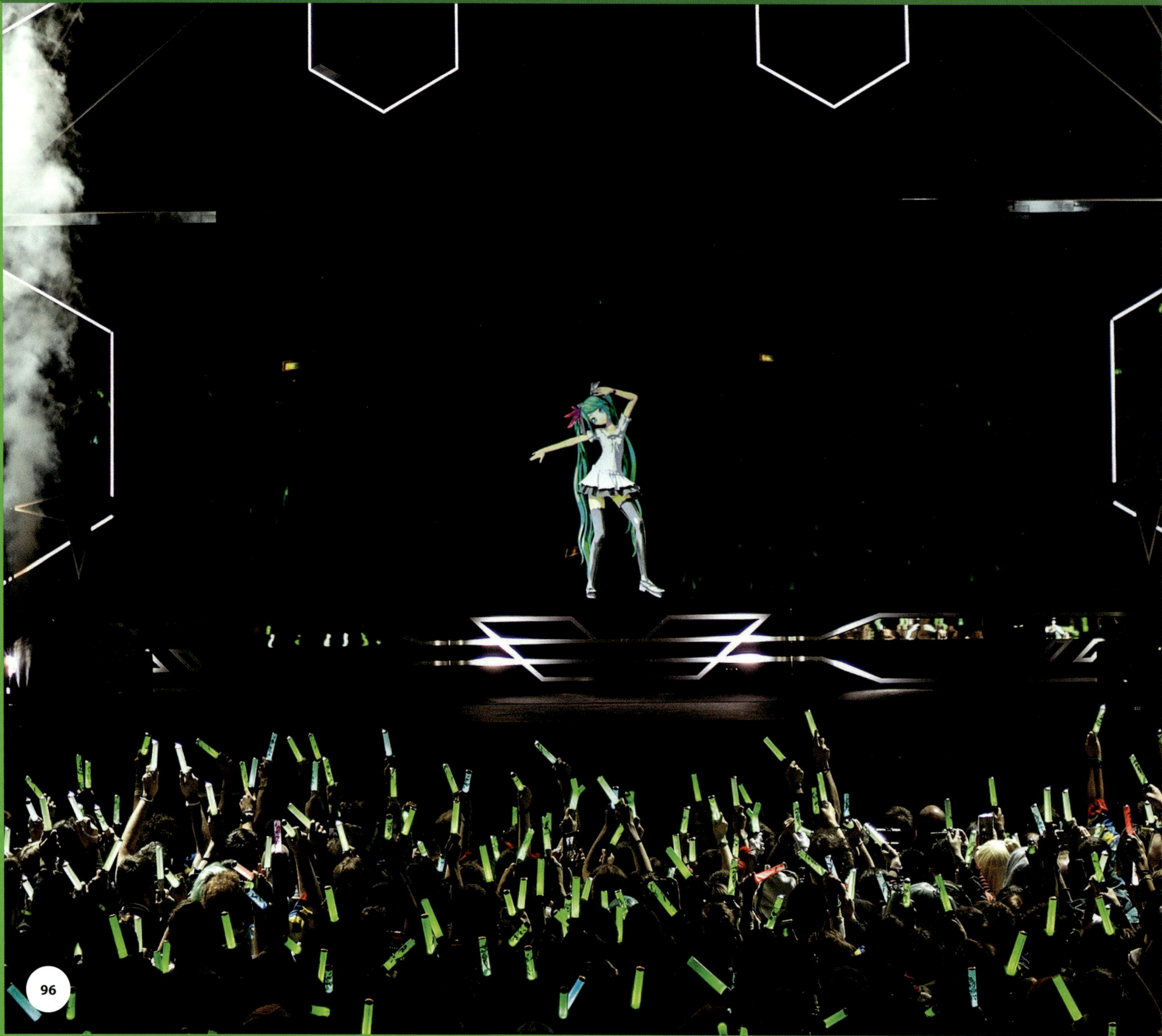

Experts predict that in the future, the music industry will see more virtual music artists interacting with fans in 3D immersive worlds. Technology is making 3D modeling more realistic and affordable. A growing number of companies, including Genies and Ready Player Me, create these models. In the future, there may also be collaborations between virtual stars and popular human musicians.

However, many people are concerned about what these changes might mean for music creators. Both major and independent labels are already signing deals with virtual artists, seeking to cash in on their music sales and virtual events. Some people worry that because there are entire teams behind virtual artists, those artists could out-create and outpace flesh-and-blood musicians.

Meanwhile, some human musicians are backing out of social media engagement. Many are stepping back from the demands placed on them by record companies as they face creative exhaustion and burnout. In 2022, British pop star Charli XCX announced she was stepping away from Twitter (since

People can attend concerts to see virtual pop star Hatsune Miku perform on-screen. In 2023, the pop star's creators announced that she'd be touring throughout North America in 2024.

> **I have been feeling like I can't do anything right at the moment. I've noticed lately that a few people seem quite angry at me—for the choices of songs I've chosen to release, for the way I've decided to roll out my campaign, for the things I need to do to fund what will be the greatest tour I've ever done.[11]**
>
> ***—Charli XCX on her reasons for reducing her Twitter engagement, 2022***

renamed X) for her mental health. She would continue to draft messages for her team to post, but she would no longer be engaging on the platform.

With so many platforms helping music creators share their work with fans, there is still room for a wide variety of artists. The world of music continues to evolve. The only constant in music is that it offers people an opportunity to create art that connects with people. Artists can keep making music that pulls listeners in and keeps them coming back for more.

Several well-known musicians have stepped back from social media. In 2023, singer Billie Eilish deleted social media apps off her phone after reading posts that harmed her mental health.

23

MAKING MUSIC PROFESSIONALLY

- The first step for a record label is discovering new artists. Representatives from the label may find artists by listening to demos, reading music blogs, exploring social media, and attending concerts.
- Once a musician has signed with a major record label, representatives of the label help the artist develop and coordinate their work.
- An artists and repertoire representative helps an artist select songs to work on. The artist writes, refines, and records those songs. They may record in a professional recording studio, where staff such as producers, managers, and sound engineers assist them. Then the songs are edited and prepared for release.
- The record label releases the artist's music through streaming services, on social media, and as physical media, such as CDs. The artist may promote their music to fans and listeners online.
- The artist performs in concerts and other events arranged by the label. This may include online or virtual events, such as *Fortnite* or *Minecraft* appearances.

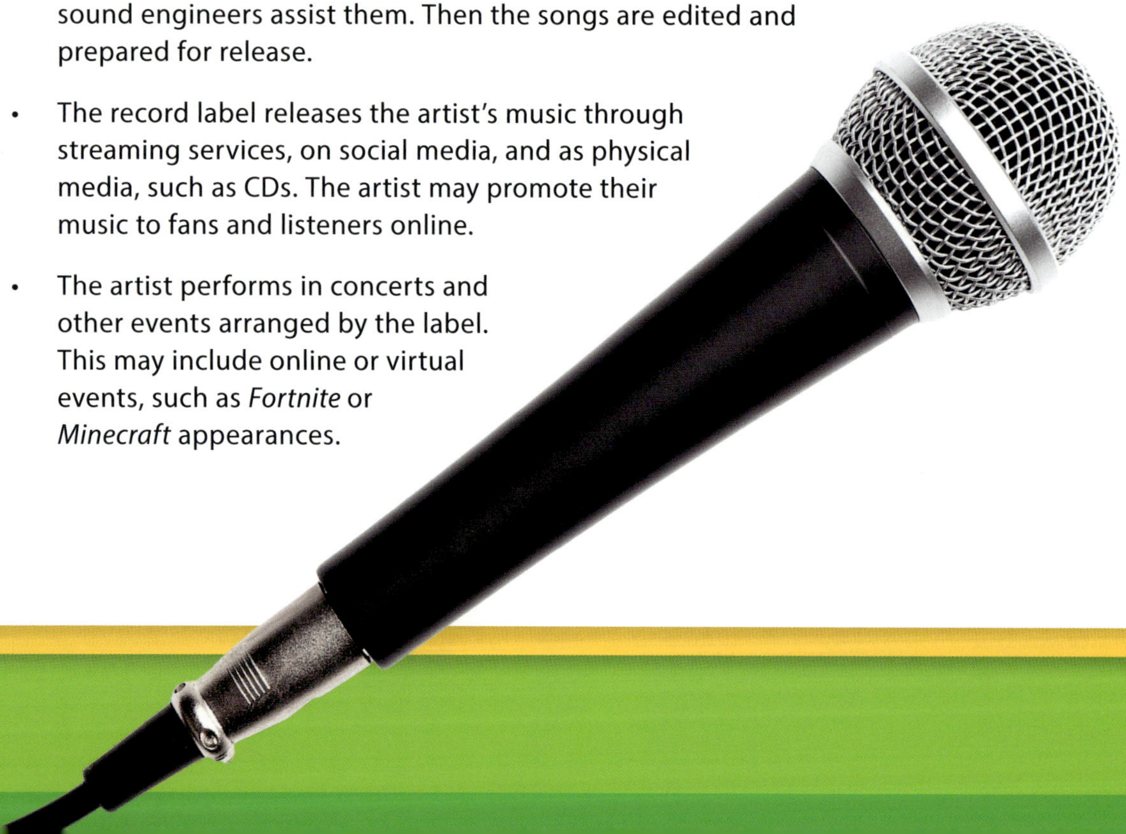

MAKING MUSIC INDEPENDENTLY

- An independent musician makes decisions about what kind of music they want to write, record, and perform. Indie artists may make and record music on their own or work with independent record labels.
- Indie artists write, refine, record, and edit their music. Many indie artists pay a distribution service to post their work on platforms and streaming services.
- The indie artist promotes and markets their own work. They may use social media, playlists on streaming services, or streaming platforms to do so. For a fee, a label service will help indie artists promote and market their work.
- Like artists with major labels, indie artists play in concerts and perform at a variety of venues.

QUOTE

"It's never been easier to release music independently, but the market has also never been so competitive."

—Tatiana Cirisano, music industry analyst, 2022

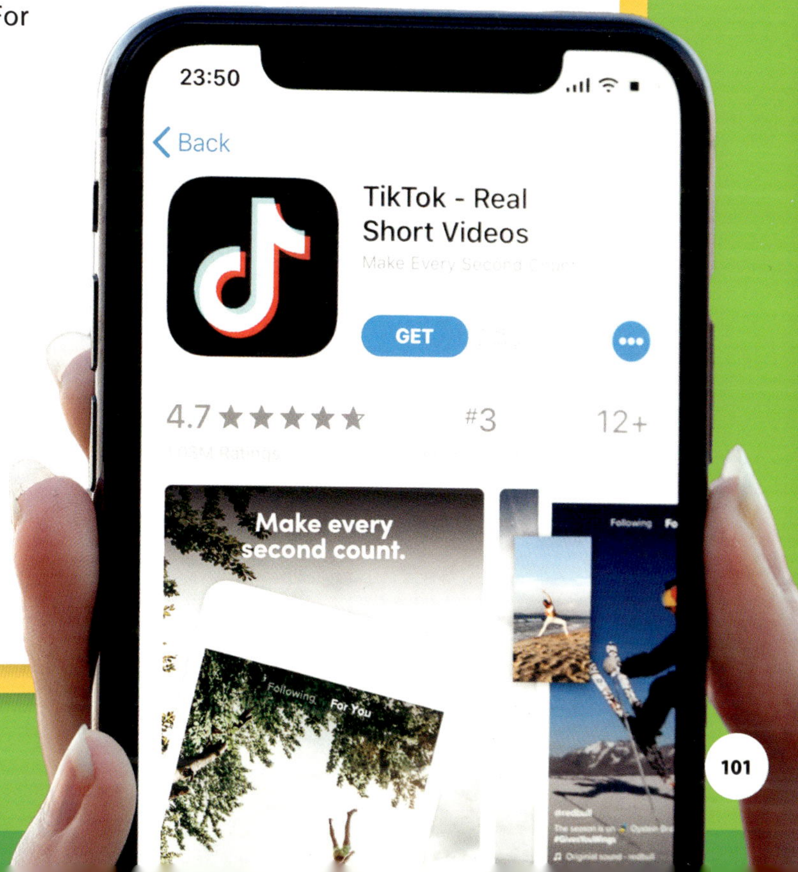

GLOSSARY

algorithm
A step-by-step set of instructions that tells a person or machine what to do.

avatar
A virtual figure used to represent a specific person.

chord
Three or more musical notes sounded together.

cuneiform
An ancient writing system in which characters are created by wedge-shaped impressions.

demo
A recording used to demonstrate how a musician plays or sounds.

extended play (EP)
A musical recording that usually includes four to six songs.

harmony
A combination of notes with a pleasing sound.

influencer
A popular content creator or social media star who has a large online following and promotes products or services to their audience.

lyre
A harp-like stringed instrument.

melody
A sequence of notes that make up the primary part of a song.

niche
Describing a type of artist or content that appeals to a specific or unique audience.

ode
A sung poem about a specific person or thing.

pitch
A quality of sound, especially how high or low the sound is.

staff
In music, a set of five horizontal lines and four spaces that runs across a sheet of music.

tempo
The speed at which a particular piece of music is played.

ADDITIONAL RESOURCES

SELECTED BIBLIOGRAPHY

"The Development of Radio." *American Experience*, n.d., pbs.org. Accessed 21 Nov. 2023.

Firth, Abigail. "d4vd." *NME*, 28 Sept. 2022, nme.com. Accessed 21 Nov. 2023.

Harwood, Mike. "Do I Need to Learn Piano for Music Production?" *Home Studio Genie*, 29 June 2023, homestudiogenie.com. Accessed 21 Nov. 2023.

FURTHER READINGS

Cross, Alan, Emme Cross, and Nicole Mortillaro. *The Science of Song*. Kids Can, 2021.

Daily, Lisa. *Pop Music*. ReferencePoint, 2020.

Jaskulka, Marie. *Making Web Content*. Abdo, 2025.

ONLINE RESOURCES

Booklinks
NONFICTION NETWORK
FREE! ONLINE NONFICTION RESOURCES

To learn more about making music, please visit **abdobooklinks.com** or scan this QR code. These links are routinely monitored and updated to provide the most current information available.

MORE INFORMATION

For more information on this subject, contact or visit the following organizations:

Grammy Museum
800 W. Olympic Blvd.
Los Angeles, CA 90015
grammymuseum.org
The Grammy Museum is home to a wide range of exhibits focused on award-winning music and artists. It hosts a variety of events, including performances and conversations with musicians.

Museum of Making Music
5790 Armada Dr.
Carlsbad, CA 92008
museumofmakingmusic.org
The Museum of Making Music teaches visitors how instruments are made and used. People can try playing a variety of instruments, including guitars, banjos, and more.

Rock & Roll Hall of Fame
1100 Rock and Roll Blvd.
Cleveland, OH 44114
rockhall.com
The Rock & Roll Hall of Fame features exhibits that explore sound, music, and the roots of rock and roll. It also hosts various musical performances.

SOURCE NOTES

CHAPTER 1. A BUDDING MUSICIAN

1. "How to Make a Cover Song Your Own." *YouTube*, uploaded by LANDR Studio, 1 Sept. 2020, youtube.com.

2. Ben Jacklin. "What Is a WAV File and How Is It Used?" *Movavi*, 7 Jan. 2024, movavi.com. Accessed 18 Jan. 2024.

3. Stephen Robles. "WAV vs. MP3." *Riverside*, 23 Dec. 2023, riverside.fm. Accessed 31 Jan. 2024.

CHAPTER 2. THE HISTORY OF MUSIC

1. Cait Miller. "Sheet Music of the Week: Let Me Call You Sweetheart." *Library of Congress Blogs*, 11 Jan. 2013, blogs.loc.gov. Accessed 18 Jan. 2024.

2. "History of the Record Industry, 1877–1920s." *Medium*, 7 June 2014, medium.com. Accessed 18 Jan. 2024.

3. "History of the Record Industry."

4. Ian Webster. "Value of $1 from 1920 to 2023." *CPI Inflation Calculator*, n.d., in2013dollars.com. Accessed 18 Jan. 2024.

5. "History of the Record Industry."

6. Devin Coldewey. "30 Years Ago, the CD Started the Digital Music Revolution." *NBC News*, 28 Sept. 2012, nbcnews.com. Accessed 18 Jan. 2024.

7. Coldewey, "Digital Music Revolution."

8. Ian Webster. "Value of $730 from 1982 to 2023." *CPI Inflation Calculator*, n.d., in2013dollars.com. Accessed 18 Jan. 2024.

9. Caroline Sullivan. "*Brothers in Arms* Popularizes the CD." *Guardian*, 11 June 2011, theguardian.com. Accessed 18 Jan. 2024.

10. Stephen Dowling. "Napster Turns 20: How It Changed the Music Industry." *BBC*, 31 May 2019, bbc.com. Accessed 18 Jan. 2024.

11. "About Spotify." *Spotify*, n.d., investors.spotify.com. Accessed 18 Jan. 2024.

12. Joshua P. Friedlander and Matthew Bass. "Year-End 2022 RIAA Revenue Statistics." *Recording Industry Association of America*, 9 Mar. 2023, riaa.com. Accessed 18 Jan. 2024.

13. Sarah Whitten. "John Legend: Music Streaming Has 'Changed Everything.'" *CNBC*, 19 June 2019, cnbc.com. Accessed 18 Jan. 2024.

CHAPTER 3. HOW MAJOR LABELS PRODUCE AND DISTRIBUTE MUSIC

1. MC WordWeaver. "How Much Do Record Labels Spend on Marketing Their Artists?" *Beats, Rhymes, & Lists*, 3 Nov. 2020, beats-rhymes-lists.com. Accessed 18 Jan. 2024.
2. "Global Music Report 2023: State of the Industry." *International Federation of the Phonographic Industry*, 2023, ifpi.com. Accessed 18 Jan. 2024.
3. "Global Music Report 2023."
4. Murray Stassen. "On-Demand Song Streams Grew 12.2% in the US Last Year." *Music Business Worldwide*, 11 Jan. 2023, musicbusinessworldwide.com. Accessed 18 Jan. 2024.
5. Dan Rys. "U.S. Recorded Music Revenues Hit All-Time High of $8.4B in First Half of 2023: RIAA." *Billboard*, 18 Sept. 2023, billboard.com. Accessed 18 Jan. 2024.
6. Alyssa Mercante. "The Reactions to *Call of Duty*'s Nicki Minaj Operator are Priceless." Kotaku, 25 Aug. 2023, kotaku.com. Accessed 18 Jan. 2024.
7. Mark Elibert. "Fans React to Nicki Minaj, 21 Savage, Snoop Dogg Coming to *Call of Duty* as Playable Characters." *Complex*, 28 July 2023, complex.com. Accessed 18 Jan. 2024.
8. "Ariana Grande Steps into the Metaverse as the Headliner for *Fortnite*'s Rift Tour." *Epic Games*, 1 Aug. 2021, epicgames.com. Accessed 18 Jan. 2024.
9. Isamu Nishijima. "Ariana Grande x *Fortnite* Rift Tour." *Medium*, 30 Aug. 2021, medium.com. Accessed 18 Jan. 2024.

CHAPTER 4. HOW INDIE ARTISTS MAKE MUSIC

1. Stephanie Sulger. "Tireless Ed Sheeran to Debut Here Friday." *San Diego Union-Tribune*, 10 May 2012, sandiegouniontibune.com. Accessed 18 Jan. 2024.
2. Anna Sky Magliola. "Ed Sheeran's Career Journey." *Planet Radio*, 13 Dec. 2023, planetradio.co.uk. Accessed 18 Jan. 2024.
3. Rachel Brodsky. "Lauren Spencer-Smith Is Gen Z's New Favorite Breakup Balladeer." *Stereogum*, 21 Jan. 2022, stereogum.com. Accessed 18 Jan. 2024.
4. Mark Savage. "More and More Musicians are Releasing Their Own Music: Here's Why." BBC, 22 Jan. 2022, bbc.com. Accessed 18 Jan. 2024.
5. Savage, "Musicians Releasing Their Own Music."
6. Savage, "Musicians Releasing Their Own Music."

7. Savage, "Musicians Releasing Their Own Music."
8. Savage, "Musicians Releasing Their Own Music."
9. "DistroKid Pricing Guide." *Sound Tech Insider*, 10 Apr. 2023, soundtechinsider.com. Accessed 18 Jan. 2024.
10. Savage, "Musicians Releasing Their Own Music."
11. Savage, "Musicians Releasing Their Own Music."
12. Savage, "Musicians Releasing Their Own Music."

CHAPTER 5. MAKING MUSIC AT HOME

1. Tim Chan. "8 Things You Need to Set Up Your Home Recording Studio." *Rolling Stone*, 6 Feb. 2019, rollingstone.com. Accessed 18 Jan. 2024.
2. Tim Ingham. "Spotify Wants 50 Million Creators on Its Platform by 2030." *Music Business Worldwide*, 30 Jan. 2023, musicbusinessworldwide.com. Accessed 18 Jan. 2024.
3. "About Yousician." *Yousician*, n.d., yousician.com. Accessed 18 Jan. 2024.
4. "Yousician Membership Plans." *Yousician*, n.d., yousician.com. Accessed 18 Jan. 2024.
5. Alper Tuzcu. "How to Open Yourself Up to Musical Collaborations." *Flypaper*, 20 Sept. 2021, flypaper.soundfly.com. Accessed 18 Jan. 2024.

CHAPTER 6. HOW INDIE ARTISTS DISTRIBUTE AND PROMOTE MUSIC

1. Glenn Peoples. "Are There Really 100,000 New Songs Uploaded a Day?" Billboard, 3 Feb. 2023, billboard.com. Accessed 18 Jan. 2024.
2. Peoples, "100,000 New Songs Uploaded a Day?"
3. Ashley King. "Are 100,000 Tracks Uploaded Daily to Streaming Platforms?" *Digital Music News*, 10 Feb. 2023, digitalmusicnews.com. Accessed 18 Jan. 2024.
4. Katie Atkinson. "Oppa! Psy's 'Gangnam Style' Video Hits 5 Billion Views on YouTube." *Billboard*, 29 Sept. 2023, billboard.com. Accessed 18 Jan. 2024.
5. Eric Dalius. "How TikTok and YouTube Have Changed the Music Industry Forever." *Entrepreneur*, 13 June 2013, entrepreneur.com. Accessed 18 Jan. 2024.
6. "Celebrating Our Thriving Community of 150 Million Americans." *TikTok*, 21 Mar. 2023, newsroom.tiktok.com. Accessed 18 Jan. 2024.

7. Ivan Mehta. "Google Says YouTube Shorts Has Crossed 50 Billion Daily Views." *TechCrunch,* 3 Feb. 2023, techcrunch.com. Accessed 19 Jan. 2024.

8. "Chance the Rapper." *Forbes*, 12 June 2017, forbes.com. Accessed 18 Jan. 2024.

9. Elizabeth Harris. "7 Short-Form Video Trends to Watch in 2023." *Leap*, 2 June 2023, theleap.co. Accessed 19 Jan. 2024.

CHAPTER 7. THE FUTURE OF MUSIC

1. Will Bedingfield. "Musicians, Machines, and the AI-Powered Future of Sound." *Wired*, 16 Mar. 2023, wired.com. Accessed 19 Jan. 2024.

2. Kyle Wiggers. "Google Created an AI That Can Generate Music from Text Descriptions." *TechCrunch*, 27 Jan. 2023, techcrunch.com. Accessed 19 Jan. 2024.

3. Jyoti Mann and Beatrice Nolan. "The Music Industry Is Freaking Out about AI." *Business Insider*, 28 May 2023, businessinsider.com. Accessed 19 Jan. 2024.

4. Wiggers, "AI That Can Generate Music."

5. Bernard Marr. "4 Ways the Metaverse and Web3 Will Transform Music." *Forbes*, 2 Aug. 2023, forbes.com. Accessed 19 Jan. 2024.

6. "AI Copyright in Spotlight After Platforms Pull 'Fake Drake' Song." *Axios*, 18 Apr. 2023, axios.com. Accessed 19 Jan. 2024.

7. "#TBT: That Time Gorillaz' Damon Albarn and Jamie Hewlett Predicted the Future." *Yahoo!*, 27 Apr. 2017, yahoo.com. Accessed 19 Jan. 2024.

8. Jem Aswad. "ABBA's 'Voyage' Virtual Concert to Go on Tour 'Around the World.'" *Variety,* 2 Mar. 2023, variety.com. Accessed 19 Jan. 2024.

9. "The Controversial Rise of the Virtual Music Artist." *Audiohype*, 11 Sept. 2022, audiohype.io. Accessed 19 Jan. 2024.

10. Lindsay Zoladz. "Hatsune Miku Is a Piece of Software. She May Also Be the Future of Music." *Vulture*, 19 Nov. 2014, vulture.com. Accessed 19 Jan. 2024.

11. Rhian Jones. "'Making Music Is about Making Assets for Social Media': Pop Stars Battle Digital Burnout." *Guardian*, 18 Feb. 2022, theguardian.com. Accessed 19 Jan. 2024.

INDEX

ABOUT THE **AUTHOR**

SUE BRADFORD EDWARDS

Sue Bradford Edwards is a Missouri-based nonfiction author who writes about culture, history, and science. She is the author of 25 other titles from Abdo Publishing, including *The Who*, *Hidden Human Computers*, and *American Life in the 1970s*. She loves a wide variety of music and sings second soprano.